THE LAYMAN'S BIBLE COMMENTARY

THE LAYMAN'S BIBLE COMMENTARY
IN TWENTY-FIVE VOLUMES

THE LAYMAN'S
BIBLE COMMENTARY

Balmer H. Kelly, *Editor*

Donald G. Miller   *Associate Editors*   Arnold B. Rhodes

Dwight M. Chalmers, *Editor, John Knox Press*

VOLUME 3

THE BOOK OF
EXODUS

B. Davie Napier

JOHN KNOX PRESS

ATLANTA

Unless otherwise indicated, Scripture quotations are from the Revised Standard Version of The Holy Bible, copyright 1946 and 1952 by the Division of Christian Education of the National Council of the Churches of Christ in the United States of America.

10 9 8 7 6 5 4 3 2

Complete set: ISBN: 0-8042-3086-2
This volume: 0-8042-3063-3
Library of Congress Card Number: 59-10454
First paperback edition 1982
Printed in the United States of America
John Knox Press
Atlanta, Georgia 30365

PREFACE

The LAYMAN'S BIBLE COMMENTARY is based on the conviction that the Bible has the Word of good news for the whole world. The Bible is not the property of a special group. It is not even the property and concern of the Church alone. It is given to the Church for its own life but also to bring God's offer of life to all mankind —wherever there are ears to hear and hearts to respond.

It is this point of view which binds the separate parts of the LAYMAN'S BIBLE COMMENTARY into a unity. There are many volumes and many writers, coming from varied backgrounds, as is the case with the Bible itself. But also as with the Bible there is a unity of purpose and of faith. The purpose is to clarify the situations and language of the Bible that it may be more and more fully understood. The faith is that in the Bible there is essentially one Word, one message of salvation, one gospel.

The LAYMAN'S BIBLE COMMENTARY is designed to be a concise non-technical guide for the layman in personal study of his own Bible. Therefore, no biblical text is printed along with the comment upon it. This commentary will have done its work precisely to the degree in which it moves its readers to take up the Bible for themselves.

The writers have used the Revised Standard Version of the Bible as their basic text. Occasionally they have differed from this translation. Where this is the case they have given their reasons. In the main, no attempt has been made either to justify the wording of the Revised Standard Version or to compare it with other translations.

The objective in this commentary is to provide the most helpful explanation of fundamental matters in simple, up-to-date terms. Exhaustive treatment of subjects has not been undertaken.

In our age knowledge of the Bible is perilously low. At the same time there are signs that many people are longing for help in getting such knowledge. Knowledge of and about the Bible is, of course, not enough. The grace of God and the work of the Holy Spirit are essential to the renewal of life through the Scriptures. It is in the happy confidence that the great hunger for the Word is a sign of God's grace already operating within men, and that the Spirit works most wonderfully where the Word is familiarly known, that this commentary has been written and published.

THE EDITORS AND
THE PUBLISHERS

THE BOOK OF

EXODUS

INTRODUCTION

The Nature of the Book

Exodus is the second book of the Old Testament. It follows Genesis, which as the first biblical book has to do with beginnings—beginnings of self-conscious, time-conscious, ordered human existence (Gen. 1-11) as well as beginnings of destiny-conscious, Covenant-conscious, and peculiarly God-conscious Israelite existence (Gen. 12-50). When we read Genesis in an awareness of what is to follow, we know that these stories of origins were created and preserved through the centuries not so much to inform ancient Israel about the past as to inform about the present; not so much to speak of what once *was* as to make clearer what now *is;* not so much to show interest in what had gone before the history of the people of Israel as to make that very history clear in its significance and meaning.

In this way, Exodus is like Genesis. It, too, is a book of origins. It tells how the people of Israel became a people and what exactly was involved in the distant opening scene of her life as a people. And like Genesis, it is a story told not out of academic interest in recovering the distant past and retelling that past for its own sake alone, but because the subsequent scenes of that history, including every "present" scene, are given sense and meaning only when viewed against this formative, exciting, and in every way remarkable first scene of the Exodus events.

Sources

We may speak and think of "sources" used in the compilation of Exodus (as also in Genesis and other Old Testament writings) if we do not make more of the matter than is justified. We may even see evidence in Exodus of three primary sources. But we must remember that we cannot always untangle them; that there is artistic and even theological meaning in the way in which sources have been combined; and that any single source is itself originally formed from lesser "sources," and is itself, therefore, a product of tradition. Thus, if we use the now standard symbols of "J," "E," and "P" to designate the three most conspicuous narrative strands interwoven in Exodus (as well as in Genesis and Numbers), we will think of "J" as the recording of early traditions which remained current and fluid down to the tenth century B.C., when the J-work was done by a single man (in this respect probably unique among the three primary sources). The symbol "E" will represent not an individual's work, but a loosely defined collection drawn from the early days of Israel's years down to perhaps the eighth century, and in its development only fixed and stopped, so to speak, by editors who combined this material with "J" to augment, to supplement, or to pose a significant variant to the "J" body of tradition. So also "P," the latest process of collection to attain fixed proportions, draws from the common mine of tradition, broad and deep, until its own fluidity is arrested when it is combined, probably by the same continuing community of priests who formed it, with "JE."

The Message

It is altogether right and appropriate that the event by which Israel became Israel should be preserved as it is here. Three major narrative strands contribute to the story, representing the mind and faith of Israel both early and late. Indeed, the Book of Exodus, more than any other single Old Testament book, stands as the testament of faith of *all* Israel. Every subsequent Israelite owned and celebrated the event as Israel's and his own creation. All the centuries of Israel's life as a political state are embraced by the telling of the story.

It is right and appropriate that Exodus comes to us as it does for another reason. Not only the *event* by which Israel became Israel is narrated here, but *that by which Israel lived* is preserved and defined. In the extensive *torah* (teaching, instruction) of Exodus, including Covenant Code, as well as Ethical and Ritual Decalogues, Israel couples with the event by which she came into being the code by which she sought to live.

Finally, and equally appropriately, Exodus preserves the record of the physical structures and objects by which the meaning of the event was kept alive and contemporaneous, and through which the *torah* was preserved and expanded.

We must always be aware of the relationship between the Exodus story and Christianity. The gospel of climactic human redemption in the event of Jesus Christ—this astonishing affirmation—derived its very form and gained its very acceptance from the ancient faith of the Old Testament that God had redeemed Israel in the event of the Exodus.

All of which is to say at the very outset of our study of Exodus that through all the centuries of the life of Israel, the people of the Old Covenant (Old Testament), and equally of the life of the Church (the New Israel, the people of the New Covenant), the events and episodes told in the Book of Exodus have been read and reread, told and retold, not so much for their "was-ness" as for their "is-ness." The ultimate goal of our study of Exodus is the deeper understanding of and commitment to our faith in him whose love daily brings us again out of Egypt, out of bondage, out of all our besetting slaveries into the land of forgiveness, renewal, redemption, and love.

OUTLINE

COMMENTARY

THE ACT OF REDEMPTION

Exodus 1:1—18:27

Israel and Egypt (1:1-22)

The Setting (1:1-7)

The first paragraph of Exodus appropriately connects the preceding narratives in Genesis about the fathers of Israel with all that is immediately to follow in Exodus about the "sons" of Israel ("Jacob"; see Gen. 32:28). These are the physical and spiritual descendants of Abraham, Isaac, Jacob, and Joseph; they are to be known collectively as Israel, the People of God.

"Seventy" (vs. 5) may be a round number. Genesis 46:8-27 lists all the names, a total of 70. The Septuagint, the Greek translation of the Old Testament, completed in the centuries just before the Christian era, lists an additional five names, which no doubt accounts for the statement in Acts 7:14 that "Joseph sent and called to him Jacob his father and all his kindred, seventy-five souls." The precise number is not important. It is of little concern that we do not know certainly whether the Greek version of the text of Genesis somehow added five names or whether the Hebrew text (from which our English translations were made) accidentally lost five names. It is the purpose of Exodus 1:1-7 to underline the fact that the total Jacob-Joseph group originally resident in Egypt was very small—simply, in terms of the ancient East, a family—but that life in Egypt was for a while benign, beneficent, and altogether blessed. This is made clear by the effective emphasis in repetition: they (1) were fruitful, (2) increased greatly, (3) multiplied, (4) grew exceedingly strong; and all to such an extent that (5) "the land was filled with them."

What land was filled with them? If Egypt is intended, then we must regard the statement as hyperbole, a figure of speech used to climax the series of words describing Israel's remarkable increase in numbers. More probably the reference is to the very small territory, Goshen, to which this family-clan was assigned (Gen. 45:10; 46:28-34; 47:1-6, 27; 50:8; Exod. 8:22; 9:26).

The earliest source of information—the oldest "record," oral or written—used in the composition of the present narratives of Exodus probably dates from the tenth century B.C. (1000-900) when the people of Israel became an integrated, autonomous political state in Canaan under the leadership of Saul, David, and Solomon. There is no question but that the state was made up of twelve dominant tribal groups already long in association. There is, on the other hand, the strongest evidence that not all of these tribes were originally involved in the actual historical experience of the exodus from Egypt. The escape from Egypt by, as will be seen, a relatively small group of slave people probably occurred in the thirteenth century B.C. (1300-1200), roughly 300 years before the compilation of the earliest fixed source which was used in the present record. There can be no doubt that Israel's earliest great historian (who, being anonymous, is known to modern interpreters by the symbol "J") understood and recounted the Exodus events in simplified, idealized terms which he applied to the original nucleus of *all* the twelve tribes in the Israelite kingdom.

We know from solid historical evidence that when the Moses group was coming out of Egypt at least some of the tribes which later became a part of the political state of Israel were already resident in Canaan; indeed, they had long been resident there. On the other hand, the record in Exodus is *in essence* absolutely true; for spiritually, religiously, theologically, *all* of the component tribes of Israel did adopt and acknowledge the Exodus event as the divine act of their redemption. All of Israel confessed, and rightly confessed, that what Israel was in essence she was because God had called her forth into meaningful existence, created her, and entered into covenant with her. As among the conglomerate people of the United States there is a common identification and a common sense of participation in the formative events of national history, so also the people of all of Israel's varied tribal backgrounds made the common confession of faith: "We were Pharaoh's slaves in Egypt; and the LORD brought us out of Egypt with a mighty hand . . . and he brought us out from there, that he might bring us in and give us the land which he swore to give to our fathers" (Deut. 6:21-23; compare 26:5-9).

This, then, is the setting. Can we make an intelligent guess as to when the Jacob-Joseph clan first came into Egypt? They were Semites; that is, they were of Semitic stock. Now the Egyptians, non-Semitic, were nevertheless ruled by a dynasty (the Seventeenth) of usurping, conquering Semites known as the Hyksos, who took over Egyptian rule about 1710 B.C. and were finally expelled from Egypt about 1570 B.C. Historians have as yet been unable to agree upon a chronological framework for patriarchal times, although there is rough agreement: the first half of the second millennium B.C. It is in every way reasonable, however, to suppose that the semi-nomadic Semites who are designated by the Jacob-Joseph name entered Egypt when it was ruled by formerly semi-nomadic Semites known as the Hyksos. If so, these few verses introducing Exodus represent a radical condensation of more than two centuries; and we can well understand the vast multiplication of the original group's numbers.

On the other hand, we have no evidence absolutely ruling out the possibility that the Jacob-Joseph group arrived during the Eighteenth Dynasty (about 1570-1310 B.C.), that is, sometime after the expulsion of the Hyksos. Semi-nomadic peoples in this part of the ancient world have from time immemorial, according to the arbitrary pressures of maintaining existence, shifted their residence from the desert and its borders to more settled but still tenuous existence in permanently productive areas of human occupation. In the second millennium B.C., Egypt always had such groups from the nearby deserts attaching themselves to her life and territory for varying reasons, in varying capacities, and for varying lengths of time.

The Turning (1:8-14)

Older historians were inclined to regard the "new king over Egypt, who did not know Joseph" (vs. 8) as a reference to the re-establishment of Egyptian rule with the Eighteenth Dynasty (about 1570-1310 B.C.). The Exodus, therefore, was usually dated around the middle of the next century, that is, the fifteenth (1500-1400 B.C.). On several counts this now appears to be, if not impossible, certainly far more improbable than a date some two centuries later. One of these reasons is considered here. Others will appear as we go along.

If it is correct, as verse 11 declares, that the Israelite slaves built Pithom and Ra-amses—and there are no good grounds to doubt it—the Exodus could not have occurred before 1300 B.C. Pithom is probably to be identified with the modern Tell er-Retabeh; excavations there confirm the fact of ambitious building in the early thirteenth century. More significantly, and with greater certainty, Ra-amses has been located at Tanis in the eastern part of the Nile delta region, in close proximity to Goshen, the territory occupied by Israel. Here excavations indicate that the city (earlier and under a different name, the capital of the Hyksos Dynasty) was destroyed in the sixteenth century when the Hyksos were expelled, that reoccupation probably began shortly before 1300 B.C., and that work went on there under the first two kings of the Nineteenth Dynasty, Seti I (about 1310-1290 B.C.) and his son Rameses II (about 1290-1224 B.C.), who gave his name to the city.

For this reason, and others which shall presently be noted, and because the weight of possible evidence in support of a fifteenth-century date becomes less and less substantial, we prefer to take the "new king over Egypt" to be just that and not the inaugurator of a new dynasty. He would be a new king who was also an intensely ambitious builder and who in consequence demanded from all of Egypt's forces of labor increased hours, an increased tempo, and more bitter, harried working conditions. Such a ruler was Rameses II. As any modern traveler in Egypt and the Near East is perforce constantly reminded, this proud monarch left his stone monuments in size and profusion over the face of his lands as none before him and none after.

Rameses' oppression was the turning for Israel. We sense that the narrative is in a sense idealized, certainly condensed; it underscores only that which was of the essence of the crisis. And this is done notably, eloquently, vividly, and with distinction: it is simply reported that the lives of the Israelites now were made bitter with hard, rigorous service (vs. 14).

The Crisis (1:15-22)

The word "Hebrew" appears prominently now (vs. 15 and following). Again it raises the question of who these people really were, and when and how they became involved in the life of the ancient Near East. The term "Hebrew" is probably related to the name of the groups who are called in the correspondence and records of Egyptian kings of the Eighteenth Dynasty " 'Apiru." The latter term is not used of a national entity, a political unit or state, but it seems rather consistently to refer to a widespread type of people practicing a communal existence. Such groups were not indigenous to the territory; they were

aliens who were able on occasion to move with effective force
on their own behalf. In Exodus the related term "Hebrew" appears for a short while with prominence, perhaps and probably
to underline the similarities in nature and function between this
group and other such groups wandering over neighboring lands
in the middle centuries of the second millennium B.C.

The group that was to become the people and nation of Israel
in the centuries following the Exodus from Egypt is described
here as a relatively unified and homogeneous entity. But it is
clear that Israel knew—and continued in her traditions to recall
—her conglomerate origins which the term "Hebrew" reflects.
In this connection Numbers 11:4 affirms that the Egypt group
was joined in the desert by a "rabble," that is, by a mixed, conglomerate multitude, no doubt long given to nomadic ways. In
the same vein one thinks of the prophet Ezekiel many centuries
later caustically demolishing the false pride of his own people
(still the same people) with this cutting reminder of their rough
and conglomerate derivation: "Your origin and your birth are
of the land of the Canaanites; your father was an Amorite, and
your mother a Hittite. And as for your birth, on the day you
were born your navel string was not cut, nor were you washed
with water to cleanse you" (Ezek. 16:3-4).

Something of the nature of this realistic reminder resides in
the word "Hebrew" which now sharply punctuates the text; but it
is not here used in any sense of shame at all. What ensues in the
full story of the Exodus is the pitting of the total resources of the
Hebrew against the total resources of the Egyptian. It is of course
God by whom victory is snatched from the seemingly vastly superior Egypt; but the form of the present story evidences huge
enjoyment of sophisticated Egypt's embarrassment and humilia-
tion through the instrument of the rough Hebrew. The Hebrew
midwives (professional persons performing the function of the
obstetrician tens of centuries before the advent and specialization
of modern medicine) do not, of course, obey the king's command
to kill all boys at birth. But when they are challenged because
of their disobedience they respond, to the great delight of every
narrator and hearer of the tale throughout the history of Israel,
in the competitive key in which the whole story is played: You've
asked the impossible! "The Hebrew women are not like the Egyptian women; for they are vigorous and are delivered before the
midwife comes to them" (1:19).

The dominant theme of Exodus is here introduced. This theme is the Lord's astounding victory over Pharaoh, the latter having at his disposal all the wealth, all the power, all the resources that man, earth, the world, and his Egyptian gods could create. It is certainly astounding, since the Lord had only himself (unknown to man, the earth, the world, and their gods) and this sad segment of Hebrews. There are secondary themes in the book, complementing the main theme, but *the theme* remains paramount, never the detailed facts which first made possible the sounding of the theme, its articulation, its proclamation, its glorification:

> Sing to the LORD, for he has triumphed gloriously;
> the horse and his rider he has thrown into the sea (15:21).

The brief paragraph in which the crisis is defined illustrates powerfully the wisdom which gave present form to the story. Here is no pedestrian enumeration of mechanical details; we have rather what is essential to the theme and what is, therefore, of enduring *meaning* at every stage in the ensuing life of ancient Israel and in the life of the New Israel, the Church of Jesus Christ.

Here, then, are the terms of the crisis. It is no photograph of the epoch but a portrait on which the artist has worked meditatively and devotedly over the centuries. The artist might be called "tradition," because with the passing of changing years and successive meaningful epochs, Israel remembered and interpreted its first exciting scene. If, in a portrait so produced, the lines of the subject have been made rather sharper than reality and the contrasts somewhat more vivid than life, it succeeds as no photograph could in eliminating the irrelevancies involved in all events in time, and highlights the essential, enduring meaning. That meaning can, in fact, be discerned most clearly only when the subsequent effects of the event are experienced, pondered, assimilated, and appropriated.

What *essentially* precipitated the action, divine and human, that resulted in the creation of a uniquely covenanted people out of a band of Hebrews existing on Egypt's edge around 1300 B.C.? Simply—and truly—the fact, the crucial fact, that their existence had become no longer life, but living death, that human life was reduced to subhuman subsistence and deprived of any characteristically human expression such as freedom, leisure, exercise of choice, the opportunity in any area, secular or religious, to be creative. "You are idle, you are idle," Pharaoh is subsequently to scream (5:17). The spark of the creatively and distinctively human is to be extinguished in these enslaved people; they are to be reduced to a living death. Such is Pharaoh's and Egypt's purpose. And if this meets with any resistance at all, which of course it does, then every son that is born to the Hebrews shall be cast into the Nile (1:22).

This in essence—though no doubt somewhat different and more complex in the literal situation—is the nature of the crisis: Egypt imposes death on the Hebrew, either in the form of minimal existence, or in the form of extinction!

Moses (2:1-25)

In a study of the narratives about Moses and the remarkable series of events in which he plays a crucial role it is important to keep always in mind two considerations.

The first is that we are dealing with a text which arrived at its present form over a period of centuries. In the course of reaching its present proportions, it has drawn from a number of sources, both written and oral—sources produced in differing times and from differing perspectives. This process by which the present Exodus came to be explains some of the characteristic and recurring features of the text.

Not at all unrelated and in some respects directly dependent upon this observation is another: namely, that Moses appears as something more than a mere man—as in the subsequent life of Israel he *was* more than a man! In very truth, for the continuing generations of the people of Israel no "photo" could embrace the form, stature, achievement, and "immortality" of Moses. In Old Testament Israel he rightly remains the first man, the *unique* man, the prophet par excellence, the peculiarly God-like man. As no other in Israel's history, Moses was given to play the role of *human* creator-sustainer-redeemer—to be sure, always employing that which God had himself provided in purpose and power. Certainly Moses was the instrument of God, the instrument by which Israel's life was itself "created"—brought out of that which was "without form and void" (Gen. 1:2) into light, into a life relatively formed, ordered, and charged with meaning and substance. Out of the chaos of the uncreated, unloved, moribund slaves, Moses was given to bring into existence a created people, loved of

God, and living to fulfill his purposes. For a man so regarded, ordinary pedestrian facts of birth and life and death (Deut. 34:6) cannot suffice to contain the man, nor indeed can they adequately represent the "truth" of the man.

Birth (2:1-10)

Under scrutiny, the text of Exodus here presents certain problems. Inconsistencies are not uncommon in Old Testament narrative literature; they ought, in fact, to be expected, in view of the process by which the Old Testament reached fixed and final form. Such internal tensions or inconsistencies were certainly evident to those who were actually involved in that process. But we have every reason to suppose that these writers and copyists and editors were relatively undisturbed by this characteristic of their maturing body of traditions.

On the other hand, people who are the products of a prevailingly analytical, logical habit of mind—possessors of modern Greek-Western modes of thinking, rather than the ancient Hebraic-Eastern quality of thought—instinctively and habitually find themselves delayed, snagged, or otherwise discomfited or dismayed by any absence in the text of specific agreement in detail, by any appearance of the inconsistent, whether overt or only implied. It is well, in such instances, to remember first of all the multiple sources and the long, fluid status of the developing text which underlie the present narratives. In addition, the unmistakable evidence is that the producers and handlers of the tradition were not themselves primarily concerned with the factual details. Rather, and always overwhelmingly, they were affirming the dominant themes, the fundamental propositions, and the *enduring meaning* of their history.

For instance, by inference (2:1-2) we would suppose that Moses is the first child born to a couple from the tribe of Levi. Yet Aaron later appears to be an older brother (6:20), and an older sister is to play a significant role in this same story (2:4-8). If the latter is Miriam (listed as the sister of Moses and Aaron in Numbers 26:59 but only as Aaron's sister in Exodus 15:20), then our sense of narrative propriety would expect the name here. Likewise in the same somewhat casual way the father and mother are first introduced in this text but only later are given names, Amram and Jochebed (6:20; Num. 26:59).

A further difficulty which we encounter here, but of a different kind, results from our knowledge of the broad life of the ancient Near East. Factual information in this respect has vastly increased in the last century, and especially in recent decades. This story of Moses' birth sounds a simple theme which appears, with variations, widely through the centuries and lands surrounding the time and place of the early Hebrews. One of the most remarkable parallels is the story concerning Sargon I, king of Assyria about 1200 years before Moses, who was said to have been set in a basket of rushes, its lid sealed with bitumen, and cast into the river, from which he was rescued by a "drawer of water."

But if similarity to the story of Moses is striking, in this and other accounts, the distinct contrast is also to be marked. In comparing such accounts one notes the relative tenderness and intimacy of the Moses account, the implicitly deep quality of human compassion and love, the unspoken but acute sensitivity to human relationships. Above all, one is struck by the meaningful irony which contributes forcefully to the central theme of Exodus, that is, the fascinating "accident" (in *Israel's* faith, of course, never a mere accident!) by which the richest gifts and endowments of Egypt are lavished upon him who will conduct the campaign which will end in Egypt's abysmal frustration. No parallels —certainly not the Sargon parallel which is commonly cited to diminish the biblical account—can exhibit all of this.

The failure of the text to measure up to *our* standards of narrative structure and coherence only emphasizes the differences between East and West. We are reminded rather sharply that any continuing relevance of this story to the life of faith is never to be found in the definition of kinship, the enumeration of names, or even the precise assignment of roles. The true meaning of the story lies in the central struggle—of gigantic significance—between God and his people on the one side, and the vigorously opposing forces which are specifically identified here as Egypt but which are also always in some measure symbolized as Egypt.

The Moses narratives, then, are certainly not a mixture of an indistinguishable pinch of history with the massive stuff of a wild, undisciplined, freely ranging popular imagination. They *are* a mixture; they are the substance of a corporate "memory." And what do we mean by corporate memory? We mean the whole process and result of a people's recall of their own past, a process which begins with memory, is continued in meditation, and is established and ended in devotion. The most complete—and from the Christian standpoint certainly the most meaningful—illustration of this kind of corporate memory and its effect in the life of God's people is to be found in the utterances of the Prophet of the Exile (Isa. 40–55).

A brief example of such corporate memory, which must have reached final form in the institution of worship, is to be found in the Hebrew confession of faith: "We were Pharaoh's slaves in Egypt; and the LORD brought us out of Egypt with a mighty hand; and the LORD showed signs and wonders, great and grievous, against Egypt and against Pharaoh and all his household, before our eyes; and he brought us out from there, that he might bring us in and give us the land which he swore to give to our fathers" (Deut. 6:21-23).

It may be—we have no way of either proving or disproving this—that the present form of Exodus 1-15 results chiefly from this same sort of interpretation of the mighty acts of God. This would mean that Israel's corporate memory of Moses and the Hebrews in Egypt underwent the long process of meditation; and the ensuing narrative was finally shaped and accented in devotional use—in the annual celebration, rehearsal, and re-enactment of the glorious event of divine creation in the triumphal exodus from Egypt. There is in such a process much that should remind us of the Church's annual memorialization of the birth, crucifixion, and resurrection of Christ.

Something like this is surely the nature of the brief story explaining the origin and upbringing of Moses. Here corporate memory has been at work over the centuries, producing what is more properly termed "history of salvation" than "history." In our common understanding of history, we mean the factual record of the past, based upon reliable contemporary evidence or documents. Tradition, while not at all divorced from history, is nevertheless basically determined by more than strictly historical concerns. Tradition is also shaped by the mind of faith, which is theology, and by the institution of worship. The result is before us in this simplified and idealized story of Moses' birth and rearing, reduced to its *essential* meaning. Its form is dictated by the first concern of both faith and worship—to render praise to God. The story is a powerful affirmation: in God's grace the very princess of Egypt is brought into the service of the Lord, of Moses, and of the Hebrews!

Identification (2:11-15a)

In these few verses Moses, in many crucial and in all outward respects an Egyptian, finds himself deeply involved emotionally with the Hebrews. In a sudden act of violence he finds himself irrevocably identified with them. To understand the focus of the narrative here we need to consider verse 11 with the preceding verse, which details Moses' name.

In the ancient East the name of a person was no mere accidental or sentimental means of identification. The name was deemed to convey the essence of the named. The name of the prophet Elijah, for example, means "Yahweh is God" or "My God is Yahweh," and it conveys the essence, the consuming passion, and the central accomplishment of the prophet's ministry (see I Kings 17-19, 21).

The interest in names in biblical times is demonstrated repeatedly, from the stories of the patriarchs in Genesis to the naming of Jesus and John in the New Testament. So important is the name, indeed, that to know the name is to know the person; to be ignorant of the name is to be as a stranger. Moses himself is later to protest the mission of deliverance with which the Lord charges him (3:13-22) on the ground that he does not know the Lord's name.

The name "Moses" is almost certainly Egyptian. It means "son" and is commonly compounded in Egyptian names such as Thutmose and Ahmose, a fact which testifies to the reliability of the substance of the tradition which remembers Moses' Egyptian rearing. Although the name is Egyptian, a Hebrew-Israelite tradition rightly records the essence of the enduring meaning of Moses' life in a naming-narrative which associates the Egyptian name with a Hebrew word meaning to draw out. The narrative specifically gives a passive reading to the name: Moses is the one drawn out, delivered, saved (from the water). But the Hebrew form of the name, literally understood, has an active sense. Thus "Moses," once brought over into Hebrew from Egyptian, means the one who executes the drawing out, and so the name points to the essence of Moses' later life and to his role of leadership in the deliverance of Israel out of bondage.

There are finely sensitive, deeply suggestive qualities of the simple narrative which we must not miss. Moses, we are to understand, had the best of two worlds: his nurse, hired by the

Egyptian princess, is his mother. In acquiring Egypt's richest endowments, he retains the best gifts of his biological family.

And now suddenly (how characteristic of tradition—but of reality too!) Moses is a man. In a single verse (2:11), in a little handful of common words familiar even to a child, all that is essential is said and all of human emotion accompanying the action is eloquently implied: When Moses was grown, he went out to "his people" (lest there be any misunderstanding, the word is literally "his brothers") and he "looked on their burdens."

Moses knows at once who he is, knows at once that he cannot, if he would, deny this identity; and he acts decisively and in violence (vs. 12). Skillfully now, and still with characteristic economy of words, the narrative reiterates the fact of this identification (vs. 13). This time (it is only the "next day") he is compassionately moved at the abuse of one Hebrew by another. Here again the primary matters of enduring meaning are stressed: Moses the deliverer is in sympathetic identification with the abused, whether tormented by an Egyptian (vs. 11) or endangered by a Hebrew (vs. 13). Moses is a man of compassion (see Num. 12:3). His irrepressible sense of identity with the Hebrew slaves, however, now compels him to become a fugitive from Egyptian justice.

Exile (2:15b-22)

Moses seeks refuge in "the land of Midian," a territory vague as to its limits because the Midianites were a semi-nomadic people. We meet them elsewhere as invaders of Canaan (Judges 6-8), and of Edom which lay to the south of the Dead Sea (Gen. 36:35). In another place (Num. 22:4) they appear as neighbors of Moab, a territory which lay east of the Dead Sea. Again (I Kings 11:14-18) Midian appears to be near the northern shores of the Gulf of Aqabah, south of and adjacent to Edom. We may safely assume, then, that Moses fled east from Egypt across the Sinaitic peninsula, probably to lands not far removed from the Gulf of Aqabah—but whether west, north, or east of the Gulf we cannot know.

Moses sat down by a well. Jacob, also a fugitive, had found a well and the beginnings of a new life (Gen. 29); in the semi-desert, as in all parched lands, life literally flows to and from the source of water. Jacob and Moses both act in a way quite out of the ordinary, and by such action win the offer of hospitality which ultimately leads to marriage in each case. The Jacob story is delightfully charged with romance and humor; the note of romance in the scene of Moses at the well is also not absent, but the plot turns on a deadly serious and consistent note—Moses' irrepressible instinct to act on behalf of the abused. Here again the stress is on Moses' character as deliverer.

The "seven daughters" report to their father the deliverance by "an Egyptian." The father is called Reuel here, but more commonly Jethro (3:1; 4:18; and repeatedly in chapter 18), and once Hobab (Num. 10:29, where the name Reuel apparently refers to the father of Hobab; see also Judges 4:11). Among possible explanations of the difference, it has been suggested that Reuel here is simply an editor's mistake at some time; or that Moses' father-in-law was known by different names in two different traditions; or that Jethro was the name in the story circulated among the northern tribes, whereas in the south the name was Hobab. In any case it is clear, since this final form of the tradition maintains three names for one man, that tradition is always interested in concerns other than the simple record of past details for the sake of the record. This kind of evidence, of course, reminds us again that multiple sources underlie our present text, although certainly we cannot always identify them.

It is a matter of significance that corporate memory recalls Moses' adopted home in Midian as the home of a priest. Moses is subsequently to be called upon to play the role not only of premier-president-commander, but of prophet-minister-priest as well. There is a strong inference in the narrative that the wisdom and hand of God are directly involved in the remarkably fortuitous circumstances of Moses' period of preparation. Indirectly (and directly, as in 18:1-27) Moses is indebted for his administrative skills, civic and religious, to Jethro, priest of Midian.

With such vigor as to reprimand his daughters, Jethro invokes the expedient but gracious principle of Eastern hospitality (the institution of the inn is a development of settled, not semi-nomadic, existence). In time a daughter becomes Moses' wife and Jethro a grandfather. The episode ends with the reminder (by means of a naming-narrative) that this good, even idyllic, life in the home of a priest may not continue. This essential point is made when the name of Moses' son, Gershom (the original meaning is obscure), is associated by his father, Moses, with the meaning "sojourner." And appropriately now the narrative points sharply back to the situation from which Moses is a sojourner, to the place and task which he cannot avoid.

People (2:23-25)

In the ancient world the sense of time was vague, and the passage of time was only approximately marked. Events widely spaced may be reported as having been contiguous, while episodes closely related may become separate. Moses remained in the home of Jethro for an indefinite, unspecified length of time. How long was he there? We cannot say, and the narrative as we have it does not specify; or, rather, it indicates both a long time and a short time. On Moses' return to Egypt, in 4:24-26, a son (the only son, Gershom?) is apparently no more than a child; and by this reckoning only a few years have elapsed. But at another point (7:7, perhaps from the latest incorporated material, commonly designated with the symbol "P," for Priestly) Moses is eighty years old when he returns to confront Pharaoh with his demands for Israel's release. Once again the positive aspects of the narrative, which speaks eloquently of the *meaning* of the days of Israel's exodus, are more important than sequential, chronological precision.

The death of an Egyptian Pharaoh during Moses' stay in Midian (vs. 23) is probably to be understood as the death of Seti I in about 1290 B.C. However, the verse could refer to the death of Rameses II, who succeeded Seti and died about 1224 B.C. All other evidence points to a thirteenth-century date for the Exodus; and this particular bit of evidence is not of such a nature as to make possible a precise determination of the date within the century. On the whole, the evidence is better satisfied on the assumption of a date early in the century rather than late. We shall assume here that the Pharaoh of the oppression was Seti I (1310-1290 B.C.), and that the Pharaoh of the Exodus was Rameses II (about 1290-1224 B.C.).

These concluding verses in chapter 2 make clear the relationship between what has gone before and what is now about to take place, namely, the call and commission of Moses. A people, Moses' people, is in bondage. Israel has cried out to God in anguished protest. God hears. God sees. God knows. Hearing, seeing, and knowing, he will act!

But a fourth verb appears in the two concluding verses of the chapter—God remembers. He remembers his Covenant with

Abraham, with Isaac, and with Jacob. Stories of the patriarchs may well have been in existence at the time, including, of course, the understanding in faith of the patriarchs as already bearing in themselves the promise to be fulfilled in and through the people of Israel. But a truly faith-full interpretation could come only sometime after Moses, when Israel had been established both as people and as nation. Israel's past influenced decisively the understanding of her present and future; but in the reverse operation of the same interpretive principles, the understanding of the present imparted new depth and meaning to the past, a new depth and meaning which it was a part of tradition's business to incorporate in the image of the past as it was being continually verbalized.

This leaves unsaid what must now be said, and said emphatically—that, given the perspective of faith, the formula of the Covenant with Abraham, Isaac, and Jacob is absolutely true. If faith is right that in very truth God himself called Israel, in order to fulfill his own purposes through her, then Israel is unequivocally justified in remembering the progenitors of Israel as themselves bearing the Covenant, themselves receiving the promise, themselves accepting the call to bless in the name of God all the families of the earth (see especially Gen. 12:1-3).

All of this firmly presages deliverance. We have had the narrative of a compassionate Moses. But this is God himself, now, who is compassionate, but more, who remembers his Covenant. Here the narrative impresses upon the hearer or reader the enormous dimensions implicit in what is happening. Here is an act of Covenant fulfillment; this is God "remembering" and so sustaining and performing his Covenant program. It is, then, a matter of universal significance and implication. This is the promise to every man and to all men who know themselves to be "in Egypt," to be in bondage. It is the promise that God hears and sees and knows—and that he *remembers!* In the moment of every human cry of anguish, in every human response to abuse, God remembers his Covenant with Abraham, Isaac, and Jacob, and his Covenant in Jesus Christ.

This is the marvel of the biblical tradition. It is formed in faith and wrought in praise of God. So formed, so wrought, it serves at its best to give classical expression in every age to every man's grateful praise for God's Covenant-deliverance.

The Lord and Moses (3:1—4:31)

Call (3:1-10)

Moses knows that he is a sojourner. He no doubt sympatheti-
cally recalls, to his own deep anguish, the miserable state of his
people in Egypt. His compassion, we assume, leaves him uneasy
and disquieted. But here he is, under the benign sun, the very
image of freedom, contentment, and peace, leading a no doubt
impressive flock to pastures along the lower mountain slopes. Is
human compassion alone ever sufficient to produce the initiative
to cut off such an existence as this, relatively protected from
coercion, from the ills of human temper, from arbitrary authority, from far-reaching and unremitting responsibility? Will human compassion alone serve to terminate such an existence in
favor of the fearfully vexed, dangerous, and apparently hopeless
role which Moses is soon to assume?

No one can diminish the stature of Moses. When full allow-
ance is made for the development of tradition, he still stands un-
challenged in the very top rank of history's great men. But the
sun on the mountains and the plains and on the woolly sheep,
the total security and satisfaction of life in the home of the priest
and in the love of his daughter—all this, under rational scrutiny
by a superior mind with superior ability to rationalize, might very
well have been retained. But this was made impossible by the
compassion and power of Another.

Horeb, the mountain of God (according to E and the Deuteronomic editors), is the same as Sinai, the sacred mountain (J
and P), which was the site of Israel's first formal act of Covenant
organization. We do not know its location. Several different iden-
tifications have been and still are urged by various interpreters,
but we must be content to leave such questions open. The location boasting the longest sustained claim is Jebel Musa, a mountain situated near the southern extremity of the Sinai peninsula.
If Jethro and the Midianites were nearby, they had ranged rather
far out of their customary orbit, east and perhaps north of the
Gulf of Aqabah; and this is by no means impossible. On the
conviction that the brilliant picture in Exodus 19, describing
God's appearance on the sacred mountain, presupposes volcanic
phenomena, some historians would locate Sinai in the territory

of Midian proper, where alone in the whole area there is evidence of volcanic action. Still others would find the sacred mountain to the north and west of the northern tip of the Gulf of Aqabah, in the area loosely defined as the wilderness of Paran. This satisfies the inference of a number of passages that the sacred mountain was not greatly removed from Kadesh-barnea, which, while not certainly identified, surely was situated just south of the Negeb (Canaan's southernmost territory) and considerably to the northwest of the tip of Aqabah.

Objections can be raised to any suggested location. The biblical evidence itself is ambiguous; for example, the notice of Deuteronomy 1:2 that Kadesh-barnea and Horeb were "eleven days' journey" apart, whereas in Numbers (13:25-29; and chapters 19-20 where, in the present order, Kadesh is named as the first stop from Sinai) no such distance is imagined. Against the plausible argument that the physical phenomena described in the narratives require a location in volcanic regions, it is countered that the same phenomena may be given a natural explanation as manifestations of violent storms. Again we must be content to accept uncertainty as to the sacred mountain's location. What is important is what faith remembers and celebrates there, and rehearses in praise of God.

We may dispense at once with the very minor problems of internal ambiguity. We understand the nature of this literature and recall again that it employs and combines elements from several sources; one strand, for example, identified the reality behind the vision as an angel, the authorized representative of the Lord (3:2); another strand speaks of the Lord himself (vs. 4). But the narrative is totally unified in what it centrally and magnificently affirms: that Moses knew, past any possible doubting, the firm call of God to "Bring forth my people, the sons of Israel, out of Egypt."

If we press the question "Now exactly what happened here?", we must turn to other similar events. What exactly happened when the boy Samuel repeatedly heard what he thought must have been old Eli's voice, only to learn and know that it was no human word, but the Word, the communicated divine nature and intent? (I Sam. 3). What exactly constitutes the literal framework supporting a prophet's word that he had received *the* Word— "Thus says the LORD"? What exactly, concretely, realistically, lies back of other radically transforming events of call, other overwhelming convictions of divine commission, such as those of Elijah (I Kings 19), Amos (7:10-17), Isaiah (ch. 6), Jeremiah (chs. 1, 11, 20), Ezekiel (ch. 1)? What, in short, is the "mechanism" by which God makes himself known to man, by which the Almighty touches the mightless, by which the Limitless penetrates the narrow confines of the limited, by which Time enters moment, by which the Holy invades the unholy, and the Word speaks in words? Even when this happens, as ultimately it did, as with finality it always does, in the person of Jesus Christ, all the forms and ingenuity of human language are inadequate to give it mechanical explanation. How much more, then, when the means of the penetration of man's otherwise impregnable little fortress-tomb, the tiny, sealed capsule of his puny life, is a Word—*the* Word? How totally impossible to describe the process initiated and executed from Without, by Another, himself quite unseen, or rather seen only in the limited form of a particular function, or to explain the breaking of the walls of the fortress-tomb, and the granting of a kind of release from the capsule! The creature to whom this happens can only cry in wonder of how this *seemed* to him, implicitly acknowledging that he tells you of what cannot be told. He *must* describe this astonishing breakthrough from Without to his within. But he describes what cannot be described. He speaks the literally unspeakable.

Moses, Samuel, Elijah, Amos, Isaiah, Jeremiah, Ezekiel—their names and number before and after are legion—know that the tightly bound, impenetrable cell of their life has been broken open. Their reactions vary; but all alike betray the sense that they are uttering the unutterable and are demanding credulity in the face of the incredible. They do not know, nor do they pretend to give back, the physical or even psychological phenomena of encounter. They mean to report in such terms, for example, as Ezekiel employs in summing up his effort to convey the experience from within his own powerfully penetrated and now devastated shell—"*Such* [he has thus far used similes in profusion] was the *appearance* [this is only how it looked and felt to me] of the *likeness* [I do not pretend to speak of the concrete reality but only of its effect] of the *glory* [this is the quality, not the substance, of the Invader] of the LORD" (Ezek. 1:28b).

About seven centuries stand between Moses and Ezekiel; nevertheless, the texture, so to speak, remains the same. Moses' initial arresting sight is a bush on fire; but it is not the mere fact

of a burning bush which intrigues him. He goes out of his way
to examine the bush when he observes that the fire continues
unabated with no change in the bush itself. As he approaches he
hears his name called and repeated. He responds simply, accepting at once the fact of an intelligent Presence, as yet unknown. The Word which is the communicated divine nature and
intent continues, saying in effect: Since I am here and you know
that I am here, since I am speaking and you are hearing, since
the Word comes into being here, since God here penetrates the
impenetrable senses of mortal man, this is holy ground on which
you are standing. You do not walk here with shoes. You stand
exposed, in immediate, unmediated contact with Holiness. In
this place of holiness where you are met, your uncovered feet
acknowledge that *you* stand all uncovered and naked in the holy
place, the tomb of your existence having been entered by the
Word of Yahweh!

To what is thus specifically preserved in memory from Moses,
faith adds the affirmation that this is the same God who spoke
the same Word to Abraham, Isaac, and Jacob, in pursuit of the
same purpose, indicating that what now is wonderfully taking
place was in truth purposed from long ago.

Such is the quality of Moses' experience of the shattered enclosure. His tiny space, the world of a moment, is exploded by
the invasion of the Fullness of Time. His word is in conversation
with the Word. His lusterless person, bared to the very core, is
engulfed in Glory.

Samuel "lay until morning" (I Sam. 3:15), surely transfixed,
incredulous, and grateful now for the quiet and the dark. Elijah
sensed the imminent invasion of his realm of the present moment as he lay huddled in the cave, and he smothered his face
in his mantle (I Kings 19:11-13). Isaiah figuratively hid his face:
in the moment of his invasion, in the overwhelming awareness
of the encompassing Glory, he cried, "Woe is me! For I am lost;
for I am a man of unclean lips" (Isa. 6:5). In quite another
sense Jeremiah hid his face. In the moment of the piercing of
his limitedness by the Limitless, in the shattering of his tight little
shell, he was appalled to find himself in the absolute nakedness
of being fully known by Another: "Before I formed you in the
womb I knew you" (Jer. 1:5). And the power and force of the
Word crashing through on Ezekiel literally felled him, so that
when he "saw it" he fell upon his face. Then the Word at length

commanded, "Son of man, stand upon your feet, and I will speak with you" (Ezek. 2:1).

Let no man be brash or flippant on holy ground, in the presence of holiness, in being addressed by the Word. Let him respond in simplicity. Let him remove his shoes or in any appropriate way acknowledge his complete knownness on the ground made holy by the meeting of Word and word. And let him always in his own way hide his face.

"Moses hid his face."

"Then the LORD *said . . .*" (vs. 7). The Word is the Lord communicating his own nature and intent. What is the nature and intent of the Lord at this holy place in the unconsuming fire? Of the human bondage against which Moses had protested back in Egypt he declares, "I have seen . . . have heard . . . I know." The Word speaks of seeing, hearing, and knowing the stuff of human bondage. The divine intent which it communicates is the purpose to deliver, to redeem.

The Four Protests (3:11—4:17)

It is God's intent to deliver Israel from Egypt. It is God's intent to bring the people forth. But who will do this? On whom, directly and immediately, will the responsibility fall? The Word to Moses is now a devastating blow: I will send *you* to Pharaoh to bring to pass the deliverance of my people Israel from Egypt!

Now Moses is not at all disposed to question the validity of the divine intention, but he has immediate and vigorous objections to make concerning the choice of personnel, namely himself. We hear him thinking that this utterly astonishing encounter has suddenly taken a wrong turn, gone sour. The Word has gone too far too fast. So Moses makes his first protest (3:11): Who is he to undertake such a thing? Moses is not merely saying, "Not I, but someone else." He is raising the serious, fundamental question of identity—Who am I? The divine response gives direct answer in the simplest possible terms: "I will be with you" (vs. 12). This, Moses, is what you have become—one with whom *I am.*

Who am I? asks Moses. Child of Israel-Egypt? Fugitive? Priest's son-in-law and Midianite shepherd? No, responds the Word. Your identity now is to be understood only in relation to Me. You are God-with-you.

Observe now the fact that a sign is not necessarily a miracle, nor even a present demonstration of some kind deemed to be immediately convincing. The sign in this case (vs. 12) is a promise that the happy outcome is already assured: that Moses, together with delivered Israel, will serve and worship God upon this same mountain. Precisely the same sense of the word "sign" appears in Luke 2:12 where, again, it is the Word which offers the sign.

Moses' problem, as is every man's problem, is believing. He wants to believe. But it is in the nature of belief to admit doubt. The coin that reads "faith" on one side reads "unfaith" on the other; and it is a coin universally possessed, and indivisible, whose two faces may not be separated or altered.

Moses accepts for the moment this definition of who he is— one who now will define himself in terms of Another. But what of this Other? Who is he? And so, reasonably enough, Moses voices his second protest (3:13-22): Who are *You?* Tell me your *name*, lest when they ask me, as ask me they will, I will have no name, and hence no real knowledge of who and what *You* are.

The earliest collection and unifying of Israel's traditions is, as we have seen, known as the "J" work (see Introduction). It apparently had its origin in the south (Judah), and it takes for granted the knowledge of the divine name, "Yahweh," from the earliest times (Gen. 4:26). Subsequent collections originating in the north or, much later still, in the Babylonian exile represent the personal name for God, "Yahweh," over against titles by which earlier he was known, as first revealed to Moses. Such is the import of the present passage as well as 6:2. It may well be that God *was* worshiped in the south by the name "Yahweh" long before the Moses-Joshua group entered Canaan, bringing with them the sacred name which only then became normative in the north. It may even be that Jethro the Midianite was more narrowly a Kenite, a member of a clan related to tribes long in residence in the south; and that the form, structure, and even the terminology of Moses' faith were influenced by this relationship. That Moses was indebted to Jethro in significant ways seems in any case certain (see Exod. 18).

But one matter becomes very clear in the present form of the story, however varied may be some of the details which it now embraces. Moses had a fresh, immediate, and convincingly unprecedented encounter with God—convincing not only to Moses himself, but of necessity (in view of what he was able to do) to the people whom he delivered.

Who am I, Lord? Who are You, Lord? A variety of answers to the second protest appears:

> Verse 14—"I AM WHO I AM," or "I WILL BE WHAT I WILL BE." "I AM" (or is the sense causative: "I CAUSE TO BE" all that is in existence?).
>
> Verse 15—"YHWH," "the LORD." (Yahweh, in the present context, is obviously taken to be related to the verb "to be," but possibly it is derived from a root meaning "to blow" or even "to sustain, maintain.")
>
> "God of your fathers."
>
> "God of Abraham . . . Isaac . . . Jacob."
>
> Verse 18—"God of the Hebrews."

The uncertainty as to the derivation of the name "YHWH" nevertheless presents always several possibilities simultaneously, all of which together testify to the nature of God. The God of the Hebrews—of this particular people, enslaved now in Egypt —is the fathers' God, the God of Abraham, Isaac, and Jacob, who *is* and *will be,* who *causes to be,* who *manifests his power* (blowing), who continues to *sustain* all life. This is the God of the fugitive Moses and of the Hebrew slave!

The outcome—to those who believe in the *name*—is assured, since the name designates the essential nature of the One who Speaks. Against Pharaoh's restraining hand it will be the Lord's mighty hand, and the slave will go forth out of Egypt arrayed in the riches of his oppressors. For the first time in Exodus, but by no means the last, we hear the note which stands in contrast to the redeeming God who, at least by inference, must be related in concern to all men. Much, much later Israel was able to speak, out of God's love, in terms of love even for Egypt and Assyria (in time to become as cordially despised in the popular mind as Egypt): "In that day Israel will be the third with Egypt and Assyria, a blessing in the midst of the earth, whom the LORD of hosts has blessed, saying, 'Blessed be Egypt my people, and Assyria the work of my hands, and Israel my heritage'" (Isa. 19:24-25). Tradition is tradition. It remembers meditatively and it preserves the totality of Israel's existence—what Israel knew and experienced of the glory of God as the People of God, intermingled with what, in utter realism, she was as a people of earth and earth's bitter passions. In subsequent commentary, both Jewish and Christian, it has been common to justify the stripping of the Egyptians (3:21-22; carried out in 11:2-3 and 12:35-36). As one of the most famous rabbinic commentators, Ibn Ezra, rationalized, even though Israel "borrowed" with no intention of repaying, reproof is out of order since all things are God's and he may therefore dispose of men's possessions as he will! St. Augustine draws a dubious, and flattering, interpretive parallel between Israel's plundering of Egypt and the Christian community's appropriation of the pagan cultural heritage of Greece. The fact is, of course, that no amount of rationalization and apology can alter the nature of the biblical tradition and record. The Word always comes with human accompaniments—until in the fullness of time, the Word became flesh. In Jesus Christ a standard was set which reveals the inadequacy and fragmentary character of the standard of behavior set forth in Exodus.

Some of the Bible's most vivid, spirited dialogue is between Moses and the Lord (for example, Exod. 32; see Num. 11). Moses, nothing daunted in his effort to evade responsibility, or at least to delay the hour of irrevocable decision, comes back with a third objection (4:1-9). Moses is almost, but not quite, saying, "This is ridiculous. You want me to go back and report all this to them. And what will their reaction be? They will say derisively, 'Listen to this! He wants us to believe that he's here on the authority of the Lord himself!'"

One almost hears the Lord say what centuries later Jesus was to say, "O man of little faith" (see Matt. 8:26; 14:31; 16:8; Luke 12:28). And doing as he is told, Moses, at least for the moment expecting nothing and totally unprepared, runs in terror from his rod-become-serpent. Two further acts are rehearsed, the leprous hand and the conversion of water into blood. Faith rightly treats the Exodus as a contest between the Lord-Moses-Israel and Pharaoh-Staff-Egypt. Egypt is defeated on her own terms—namely, a magician's apparent power over the objects of his environment. Inevitably memory highlights and no doubt augments this thematic motif. Did Moses *in fact* enter the arena, so to speak, with Pharaoh's magicians? This we have no reason to doubt; but we should at the same time be skeptical about our competence to reconstruct with any historical precision the actual external details of the original contest.

As the narrative turns immediately to Moses' fourth and final protest (4:10-17) Israel's estimate of Moses is particularly clear.

It is no false, oriental courtesy-modesty out of which Moses speaks. This man's humility goes deep. He regards himself in truth as insufficiently qualified for so gigantic a task. Well may it be recorded of him that he "was very meek, more than all men that were on the face of the earth" (Num. 12:3).

But now Moses pushes the divine patience too far. It is not simply, however, that he protests his lack of eloquence, his poor verbal facility; he feels constrained to add that he, Moses, has noted no improvement in this fundamental handicap during this present remarkable confrontation by God. Even this unprecedented interview with the divine Presence, this audition with the Word, effects no change.

The answer of the Lord is double-pronged. The first is an unequivocal, even stirring affirmation of the biblical creation-faith, the faith in the absolute sovereignty of God as Creator and Sustainer of the life, the time, and the total environment of man. The second prong of the response acknowledges, it would seem, the validity of Moses' protest—but overcomes it in the affirmation, "I will be with your mouth and teach you what you shall speak" (vs. 12; see also the similar exchange between the Lord and Jeremiah, Jer. 1:6-7).

Now comes the verifying climax. Moses speaks, on top of all this, his most tactless, ungracious, even disrespectful line. It is worse than the translation of the Revised Standard Version suggests, "Oh, my Lord, send, I pray, some other person" (vs. 13). To interpret and paraphrase, Moses shrugs as he says rather insolently, "You have my permission. Send whom you please! I'm not your man!"

It is no wonder that later records, faced with the puzzle of Moses' failure ever to enter the Land of Promise, return the verdict that it was because he "spoke words that were rash" (Ps. 106:32-33; compare Num. 20:10-13). Nor is it strange that the Lord is now represented as angry (4:14). But it surely remains through all ages a matter of comfort to lesser men deploring their own lack of faith that Moses, the central figure of Old Testament history, on the occasion of his call—and in the face of overwhelming assurance of divine endorsement and support—acted in unfaith!

Many present-day interpreters of Exodus would see Moses and Aaron in a kind of typological treatment (as, in this case, the first representative of two subsequently emergent types). Moses typifies the prophet; Aaron represents the priest. Whatever the original circumstances giving rise to the story, the relationship of Moses and Aaron is so presented as to define the proper status of the one type or functionary as over against and in relation to the other. Moses is the prophet, Aaron the priest. In the fixed, final form of the story as it comes now to us, the relationship is cordial, and the two functions are deemed to be mutually dependent. It is the role of the prophet to receive the Word and convey it to the priest: "You [Moses the prophet] shall be to him as God" is the Word to Moses. But the implementation of the Word is the priest's responsibility: "He shall speak for you [Moses] to the people" (vs. 16).

Now this is interesting, and it is no doubt a fruitful way of looking at such texts. It is, nevertheless, necessary to speak very cautiously in the matter of how, in any specific instance, the earliest form of the tradition has been modified by subsequent reading back. Again we cannot be absolutely sure of methods and details, but are confident that by and large the essential meaning is preserved in the record of the significant past. What is in essence remembered, and rightly remembered, is that the institutions of Israelite prophetism and priesthood were present in the people's history from the very earliest times, and that they developed together in the closest kind of relationship. (Besides Moses, two other dominant figures of relatively early times, Samuel and Elijah, combine in themselves marked qualities of priest as well as prophet.)

So the narrative leaves us with the impression that the persistently protesting Moses is finally overridden, as he subsides before the powerful Word and God's assurance of competent, even eloquent assistance from Aaron.

Reaction and Response (4:18-31)

When we read these portions of the narrative in Exodus with any care at all, we are frequently made aware of the underlying process by which they developed and of the several sources which were more or less obviously involved. This process is particularly apparent in 4:18-31. The order in verses 18-19 indicates the process. Moses gains Jethro's blessing for a return to Egypt without referring to the Lord; and *then* receives the Word of Yahweh to return. In verse 20 he takes his wife and sons (plural), although we have previously been informed of only one son and

in the immediately following episode (vss. 24-26) only one son
is presupposed. Verse 20, moreover, apparently returns Moses
all the way to Egypt with wife and sons without interruption.

But verse 21 seems to go back for its sequence to verse 19.
The Lord gives further instructions, clearly prior to Moses' departure. The episode at a "lodging place on the way" back to
Egypt follows; then Moses' and Aaron's meeting at the "mountain of God"; and, finally, Israel's acceptance of their leadership,
and the people's worshipful response to the mediated Word of the
Lord. In short, what we are given here, in a sequence perhaps
somewhat disturbed, are nevertheless the most significant items
lying between Moses' call and the start of his program of deliverance (5:1-3). The account also indicates that considerable
time had elapsed since Moses first came to Midian from Egypt
(vs. 19).

Moses' recently bestowed powers will not of themselves effect
deliverance (vs. 21); inferentially, we understand already that
this can result only from the efficacious Word of the Lord.

Pharaoh is to be informed (vss. 21-23) that Israel is the Lord's
first-born son (see Hosea 11:1, "my son") and that Israel is to
be released for only one cause—"that he may serve me." This
becomes a demand-theme, to be repeated in the coming chapters
again and again: Let my people go that they may serve me!

If release is refused, judgment will be in kind; the punishment
will fit the crime (vs. 23b). The negative judgment will be utterly
appropriate: for this "death" of the Lord's first-born there will
be the death of Pharaoh's first-born. (This early standard of
justice of an eye for an eye is later superseded in both Old and
New Testaments.)

In a strange little narrative (vss. 24-26), surely reaching back
in its present form to a time not far removed from the Mosaic
era itself, Moses' brush with death—by illness or by accident—
is recounted; and it is the verdict of the earliest strand of the
record that Moses' serious condition was the occasion for the
performance of the rite of circumcision as the outward sign of
commitment to the Lord's promise and purpose so that commitment was sealed, as it were, in blood. This is illustrative of the
whole concept of Covenant, combining divine Word and human
response: the disclosure by the Word of divine nature and intent,
and man's acceptance in faith (here testified to in circumcision)
of that Word. The circumcision is performed on Moses' son but

vicariously upon Moses; and this act of Covenant-making effects the cure of Moses' sickness-unto-death. This calls to mind, of course, other Covenant narratives (Genesis 15 and 17, for example) as well as the New Covenant sealed in Jesus Christ, to which millions upon millions have testified as the healing of their sickness-unto-death.

In a final scene in this series Israel's initial response of unqualified faith is stressed: "And the people believed . . . they bowed their heads and worshiped " (vs. 31). God's mighty word brought about Israel's deliverance from bondage, from chaos, from meaninglessness. But this mighty deliverance followed only upon the response of faith from within the life of bondage, chaos, and the meaningless!

The Lord, Moses, and Pharaoh (5:1—15:21)

There is repeated evidence through this section of material from the three "sources" J, E, and P. But we will not let the trees obscure the forest. One is not to seek for the separate meanings of such sources, but for the remarkably unified affirmation of faith found in the combination as it stands. However, for the sake of an intelligent understanding of the present text and its occasional mild disorder or repetition, we observe first that whereas JE appears through 6:1, the Priestly history is markedly present in 6:2—7:13.

The Preliminary Meetings (5:1—7:13)

The issue is at last joined. Pharaoh is confronted with God's demand, "Let my people go, that they may hold a feast to me . . ." (vs. 1; a variant on the theme to be repeatedly sounded, "that they may serve me"). The response is natural: "Who says so? Whose word is this? Who is the Lord?" The inference is clear: I never heard of him! The answer is definite: No!

The language of the dialogue remains colorful, vigorous, and imaginative. The direct demand has failed. As if in partial answer to Pharaoh's question, "Who is the LORD?" the demand now comes more gently with a subtle appeal to Pharaoh's pity for a people about to be judged for their disobedience (vs. 3). But Pharaoh is quite beyond such an appeal. A people already lazy (an alternate reading of the phrase, "the people . . . are now many") and without enough to do (vss. 8 and 17) are using the occasion of this vain request to avoid further work! By increasing their labor Pharaoh will help them forget any foolish notions of freedom. Let them continue to produce bricks in equal number, but now without straw. Let them scavenge for their own cohesives!

The Israelite foremen bitterly protest to Pharaoh, who repeats the brutal allegation, "You are idle, you are idle," and in cruel sarcasm mimics Moses, or possibly Aaron: "Therefore you say, 'Let us go and sacrifice to the LORD'" (vs. 17). In language which verges on cursing, he dismisses them. Shamed, smarting, frustrated, they run into Moses and Aaron on their way out and let fly upon them their sense of outrage in strong terms which can be understood in all time and in every language: "You have made us stink!" (the literal meaning of "you have made us offensive" in 5:21). And Moses reacts as he is to react again and again in the face of such personal bitterness. He turns to the Lord and he is reassured.

There is now recorded an alternative tradition of the call of Moses or a renewal, at a critical moment, of the call experience (6:2-9). It brings to mind the earlier episode of the mountain of God, the burning bush, and the holy ground (3:1-6). But the setting now is Egypt, and there is no attendant vision. The sense of the awesome and the mysterious in the earlier scene gives way here to theological assurance and eloquence. Here a highly articulate Word gives fluent expression to the nature and purpose of the Lord. In the prior account the sense of Covenant is only implied (although still emphatic), but the term itself is conspicuous here.

It is nevertheless the *same* Covenant. It is the same Word. It is the revelation of the *same* divine name (6:3) made first to Moses. It is a sure and fine stroke which repeats in essence Moses' radically transforming encounter with the Word at Horeb: now, at this moment of abysmal discouragement, immediately after the totally frustrated first appearance before Pharaoh and the bitter verbal abuse from the Israelite foremen, the Word comes to him again. Moses, we think, could have continued at all *only* in the power of a renewal of purpose effected by this vivid reappropriation of the Word which first moved him from Midian to Egypt.

And the language! The Priestly material has its long and boring genealogies (for example, 6:14-25); it embraces giant blocks

of legal material; it sometimes betrays (to our tastes) an un-
necessarily minute interest in the external accouterments of institutional religion. But it also incorporates some of the Old
Testament's most beautiful and eloquent theology. The moving
word to Moses in 6:2-8 should be read aloud. Its form suggests
strongly that it had existed for generations as a spoken liturgy
or confession of faith, habitually recited from memory in the
rhythm of formalized worship. Note also in the reading that this
is the *word*, it is what God *said* to Moses; that the quality of
divine compassion and mercy and grace here comes through as it
has not previously in Exodus; that this is a recital of faith in the
nature and purpose of God (see the emphasis upon the divine
"I," even more pronounced in Hebrew, and compare the same
feature in Joshua 24); and that all of this is an expansion of the
single, simple, eloquent theme which opens and closes the recital: "I am the LORD," conveying in the very name all the essential meaning of the divine Life.

In terms still reminiscent of his earlier encounter with the
Word, Moses protests again. It is the same fundamental protest.
This time, however, after Moses has experienced an initial failure
both with Pharaoh and with his own people, it is a protest with
the authority of experience behind it. Even my own people will
not hear me, he says in effect (6:12); how can I expect any
results in speaking to Pharaoh with my "uncircumcised lips,"
that is, with this covered, bound, constrained, muffled, thwarted
speaking mechanism. I need radical surgery on my mouth!

This *may* be a parallel account to the narrative of the call in
3:1-6. The issue remains finally undetermined; but it is clear
that the process which brought about this final form of the text
out of tradition's multiple sources was itself inspired. This moving episode between Moses and the Word moreover has the
quality of psychological and emotional authenticity; its vastly
strengthened language of protest is an appropriate response to
Moses' apparently abject failure in his preliminary meetings with
Pharaoh and with Israel's representative foremen.

The genealogy of 6:14-25 appears to interrupt the scene which
breaks off at 6:13 and resumes, apparently, at 6:28 to continue
through 7:9. It is, however, no real interruption. On the contrary, it is necessary now to ask the questions which are important in the ancient East: Who, after all, are Moses and
Aaron? Who are the Levites? Who are these in terms of the

names and persons from whose very loins they came? We must know who they *are* in terms of who they *were!* The answer to these questions also establishes the ancient authority and legitimacy of all subsequent priests and of the very institution of the priesthood. This is (except for verses 14-15; compare Gen. 46: 9-10) Levite genealogy, concerned to say who Moses and Aaron were. But the emphasis genealogically is finally on Aaron (through whom, and not Moses, the line continues) and implicitly on the institutional priesthood. In the genealogy Moses and Aaron—who incidentally are placed four generations removed from Jacob—are clearly identified: "These are the Aaron and Moses" who are so involved in the Exodus (6:26).

Moses repeats his deprecatory self-criticism: his lips are uncircumcised. The response of the Word this time is: You will be to Pharaoh "as God" (not Yahweh!)—that is, so far as Pharaoh is concerned you will possess certain attributes of deity. You need, then, have no fear! And Aaron shall be your prophet; that is, he will be your spokesman (as the great prophets of the Old Testament are essentially the Lord's spokesmen, or perhaps more exactly, spokesmen of the Word, deliverers of the Word, proclaimers of the Word, and even actors of the Word). In the following verses (7:2-5) the proposition of faith is reaffirmed that what is done in Egypt for Israel is done also for the Lord—that even the Egyptians may know that he is the Lord (vs. 5).

The chronology of Moses' life presents difficulties (vs. 7). He is represented elsewhere, in what may be an idealized pattern, as having survived three standard generations of 40 years each, in three distinct phases of equal length: 40 years each in (1) Egypt, (2) Midian, (3) Wilderness (see Deut. 34:7 and Acts 7:23, 30).

In verses 8-13, again perhaps indicating that there has been a combination of more than one report, Aaron wields the rod endowed with magic powers before Pharaoh and his staff of world-renowned magicians (not Moses, as in 4:2-4, 17). The trick is promptly duplicated by the whole complement of Egyptian magicians, but the story adds quickly that Aaron's rod-into-serpent swallowed up the Egyptian equipment!

Still Pharaoh's heart was hardened (7:13). Still pride and ambition were unmoved. Still power remained totally corrupted by power. Still the world turned a deaf ear to the cry of faith. Still the deification of man thwarted the freedom that is to be found only in worship of God.

The preliminary meetings were all abortive.

Nine Plagues (7:14—10:29)

Toward the softening of Pharaoh's heart and to the end that a people may be released from human bondage for the perfect freedom of God's service (see the refrain, "Let my people go, that they may serve me," in 7:16; 8:1; 8:20; 9:1; 9:13; compare 10:7; 3:12; and 4:23), nine wonders occur:

1. Water becoming blood, 7:14-25.
2. Frogs in unheard-of numbers overrunning inhabited Egypt, 8:1-15.
3. and 4. Insects in unprecedented profusion, 8:16-32—gnats, verses 16-19, and flies, verses 20-32.
5. Wholesale destruction of Egyptian cattle by plague, 9:1-7.
6. Widespread affliction by boils, so severe as to render the Egyptian magicians' continued appearance impossible, 9:8-12.
7. A fearfully destructive hailstorm, 9:13-35, from the effects of which the Israelites are spared by miracle (vs. 26) or foresight and precaution (vss. 18-19).
8. Locusts, 10:1-20, in such numbers as to "cover the face of the land" (10:5) "so that the land was darkened" (10:15), and to "eat every plant in the land," all that the hail had left (10:12).
9. Three days of thick darkness, 10:21-29, "a darkness to be felt" (10:21).

Now here again it is quite impossible to know the exact details of what happened. There are three major strata of tradition mingled here; no single stratum appears to have recorded all nine wonders; and some could well be duplicates—the third (P?) and fourth (JP), for example, both being plagues of insects; or eighth and ninth, both being plagues of darkness. At the same time any interpretation must take into account the confessional form of this tradition; that is, that its present structure, intent, and emphasis are derived from its use in worship and its repeated recitation throughout ancient Israel's generations during annual celebrations of the great deliverance. The whole unit in which this passage stands (Exod. 1-15) is the product, on the one hand, of a considerable literary development and, on the other hand, of a relatively uniform liturgical tradition.

At the same time there is no good reason to doubt that the essence of the major historical episodes is preserved. If the oc-

currence in Egypt of hail and locusts in catastrophic severity is
rare, plagues of frogs, insects, and always related diseases are a
repeated phenomenon of Egypt's history. The waters turned to
blood reminds us that when the Nile begins its annual rise, red
dirt from the mountains of Abyssinia colors the water. And
darkness over the land has for centuries periodically occurred as
a result of violent sandstorms.

But to pass this narrative off merely as accurate history is
grossly to misinterpret it. We, along with the recorders of ancient
Israel's tradition, may well understand that Israel's escape from
Egypt followed immediately upon and indeed in consequence of
an uncommon series of "natural" disasters. But this alone obviously would never have resulted in the preservation of the
"memory" and the continued celebration of the event in the annual religious festival. What is preserved in this tradition—and
it is as firm, as concrete, a historical datum of the event as is the
role of Moses—is the fact of the *faith* of the participants. This
faith is shared, but certainly not "read back," by the ones who
recorded the events; it is the faith that the calamities falling with
such severity upon Egypt were occasioned and controlled by the
Word, God's Word. This was God's action, disclosing his nature
and purpose—his nature as Lord of creation, and his purpose
to make of Israel a people. And always implicit, of course, in
making Israel into his people is the ultimate mission of making
all nations his (see Gen. 12:3; the symbolic inference of Gen.
41:57; and, as examples only, Isa. 2:3; 11:1-9; 19:23-25; 49:6).

To this theme—the expression of faith in the basic nature and
meaning of the event of the Exodus—all else is subordinated.
Thus the final form of the narrative is not marked by exact con-
sistency. (For example, is all of Egypt's water affected, 7:19
[P?] or only the Nile waters, 7:17-18 [J?]?) And the roles of the
major characters are drawn in idealized, typified, simplified fashion, with greater interest in theological meaning than in historical
function. Most conspicuous in this regard is the role of Pharaoh,
who served as the type of unfaith—brought repeatedly to the
brink of submission, but never voluntarily won—and ultimately,
therefore, the victim of crushing defeat.

It would be impossible to say what role was actually played by
the Pharaoh, probably Rameses II (about 1290-1224 B.C.). The
extremely powerful significance with which the event of the
Exodus is charged in the narrative accurately and appropriately

reflects Israel's rather than Egypt's estimate. Since it is mentioned nowhere in contemporary Egyptian records thus far uncovered, we may assume that it was, from Egypt's perspective, nothing remotely resembling the momentous event it seemed to be to Israel. But from Israel's point of view—since this event marks her birth as a people, her very creation out of the formless and the void—exaggeration is impossible. So we understand the tendency and even the necessity of representing the Exodus as also of crucial consequence to the very person of the Pharaoh of Egypt! To remember it in any other way would be to distort the true significance of the event by diminishing it. What is recorded is spoken out of faith and in testimony to faith; and what is thereby conveyed of fundamental significance is in this sense profoundly true! Pharaoh's role and response in this event of the Word's action is, to the mind of faith, authentic. "Let my people go, that they may serve me!" The answer of Pharaoh—demonstrating unfaith, pride, arrogance, idolatry, greed, ambition—has been and always will be to the effect that these are not "your" people, but "mine"; they may not serve you, they must serve me!

Yet One Plague More, and Religious Feasts (11:1—13:16)

The narrative here begins in the midst of Moses' last interview with Pharaoh, following the ninth plague. Pharaoh is trying in bitter anger to dismiss Moses; he threatens that if Moses looks on Pharaoh's face again, it will cost him his life (10:28). Moses concurs: "As you say! I will not see your face again" (10:29).

This is the dramatic introduction to the tenth plague. It is not yet the end of the interview. In 11:1-3 the parenthetical comment is inserted that this last plague will not only effect release but that Israel will be driven out; and that, because of the high esteem in which Moses is held among Egyptians and the (implied) cordial relationships prevailing between Hebrew and Egyptian, the people of Israel will leave wearing the valuables of their Egyptian neighbors—a somewhat milder though not essentially different form of the theme sounded in 3:22.

Moses' final interview with Pharaoh continues at 11:4. It has come now to this: Pharaoh has continued to refuse life—that is, freedom to serve God—to the Lord's first-born (4:22-23). He will now experience the appropriate judgment—the death of his and Egypt's first-born, including even cattle (11:5; see also that remarkable, tender phrase which concludes the Book of Jonah, ". . . and also much cattle" in Jonah 4:11). As in the earlier narrative of the plagues, there is sounded again the great cry "such as there has never been, nor ever shall be again" (vs. 6). Israel knows herself to be the creation of the Word of the Lord, and that whole event was such as had never been, nor would ever be again.

The contrast between Israelite and Egyptian, also a common motif in the accounts of the other plagues, appears again in a brilliant figure of speech: while death moves at midnight against every first-born creature in Egypt, the Israelites will not even be subjected to the growling of a dog! All of this is detailed in Moses' final speech, which concludes in a fury of words. When this night is over, he says to Pharaoh, the Egyptian people "shall come down to me, and bow down to me, saying, 'Get you out, and all the people who follow you.' And after that I will go out" (vs. 8).

In the course of the Israelite religious year the most prominent and probably the oldest festival was the Passover, which, from the time of Moses on, was celebrated in the spring of the year in commemoration of the Exodus from Egypt and particularly the "passing over" of the Israelite homes when death invaded Egypt and claimed her first-born (see 12:23). The core of the festival —no doubt known by some other name—may well have been much older than the thirteenth century B.C., originating among pastoral people as a spring celebration of the birth of the lambs, with appropriate attendant rites for the consecration and protection of the flocks, and probably a communion meal shared by the shepherd group and its deity. (Exodus 5:1 probably refers to such a feast, the parent festival, so to speak, of the Passover.)

There is recorded here, together with the account of the tenth and decisive plague, the full prescription for the Passover celebration (12:1-13, 21-27, 43-49). A second, closely associated festival, the Feast of Unleavened Bread, is also given its first prescription here (12:14-20; 13:3-10). In subsequent centuries, when Israel had become an agricultural as well as a pastoral people, this agricultural festival also commemorated the Exodus (12:17; 13:8). And a third annual religious rite is introduced now in conjunction with this climactic episode in Israel's deliverance—the rite of the dedication of the first-born (13:1-2, 11-16; see also the further elaboration in Numbers 3:11-13, 40-

51; 18:15-16). Its introduction here has also an obvious appropriateness in its association with the moving "first-born" theme which dominates the entire episode.

The first simple Passover was no doubt celebrated in a form which was deemed by the participants to be related in a real sense to their escape. But the narrative gives us a form of celebration developed over the seven or eight following centuries (12: 21-27 appears to be derived from the older J stratum; but 12: 1-13, 43-49 is of the character of the Priestly history), since this developed meaning alone can represent the episode's true significance. Much the same thing is to be said of the other two associated rites, that of unleavened bread, and that of the dedication of the first-born. Indeed, both of these may have been of later origin; but the developed, regularized rites effectively convey that which Israel in faith continued to hold as the central meaning of her birth-night: God made himself known as Lord of life and creation, of time and history. In transforming an agricultural festival which originally may have celebrated the fertility of nature into a ceremony memorializing the action of the Lord's Word in history, Israel underscored her faith in the purposive reign of God in time and history. In relating the rite of the dedication of the first-born to that same momentous night, she declares this meaning in her deliverance from Egypt: the same Lord who brought her forth gives and sustains—and so rightfully owns and possesses—all life!

Escape by the Sea (13:17—15:21)

This episode can most conveniently be surveyed in four sections. In the first (13:17—14:4) Israel begins her exit unchecked by Egypt.

There is conflict between 13:17, "Pharaoh let the people go," and 14:5a, "When the king of Egypt was told that the people had fled." The latter seems to presuppose that only now is he informed of their escape. In either case, of course, one thing is clear: Israel fully expects pursuit.

Israel does not take the direct route to Canaan "by way of the land of the Philistines." This is, of course, an anachronism— that is, a form of reading back—since the Philistines probably did not occupy Canaan's southern coastal strip until several decades after the entrance of the Moses-Joshua group. This way is the way of the broad "highway" which ran eastward and then northeastward along the Mediterranean coast. It was the easiest and shortest route, to be sure, but also the most hazardous both with regard to departure from Egypt (Egyptian pursuit) and with regard to entrance into Canaan (vulnerability to attack from local inhabitants). The complete narrative of Israel's experience offers a number of explanations for the long delay in the occupation of Canaan; but, for all the variation in detail, there is the emphatic understanding that Israel was, in leaving Egypt, totally unprepared for the difficult and highly hazardous task of entrance and occupation of a new homeland. Here, for example, in verse 17 we see a people not merely materially unprepared for violent skirmish, but psychologically so tenuously committed to the present enterprise as to give it up at the first hostile bark of a dog. We shall presently see this judgment strongly reinforced. That Israel, therefore, went out "equipped for battle" (vs. 18) seems quite impossible; and it may be that we ought to read the text here, as suggested by many interpreters with good reason, "by fifties" or "in five divisions" (referring to the organization of the march).

The "Red Sea," first mentioned in 10:19 and again here (13:18) and repeatedly hereafter, is a consciously erroneous rendering of a Hebrew term by nearly all translators from the time of the Septuagint (third century B.C.) through the Authorized Version of 1611, to the Revised Standard Version (1952). The mistranslation continues to survive, presumably because of its now classical status, as it were. To speak of Israel's phenomenal deliverance at any other sea than the "Red Sea" does shock the long-conditioned ear. What is translated "Red Sea," however, is not Red Sea but "Reed Sea" (not such a shock to the ear after all), or "Sea of Reeds." For well over half a century, moreover, no biblical commentators, historians, or geographers of note have argued that the sea in question is the Red Sea, that is, the Gulf of Suez. On the other hand, it must be admitted, this distinguished company has as yet been unable to achieve any significant measure of unity on the actual identity of the "Reed Sea"—other than in the astute observation that it must have been a body of water in which reeds commonly grew! Some would make it Lake Sirbonis, east of Egypt and adjacent to the Mediterranean; but this lies almost directly on the way by "the land of the Philistines." More commonly it is identified with one of several bodies of water now lying, or at one time lying (the Suez

Canal has at points radically altered the topography of the strip),
along the course of the Suez Canal between the Gulf and the
Mediterranean. The crossing would have taken place, then, perhaps at the northern end of Lake Timsah (in the southern half
of the strip), or perhaps at the southern tip of Lake Menzaleh to
the north.

The difficulty of locating the Reed Sea with any certainty is
enhanced by the fact that closely associated place-names have
not as yet been positively identified. In 12:37 it is noted that
escaping Israel moved first from Ra-amses to Succoth. If we accept the identification of Ra-amses as Tanis in the southeastern
part of the broadly spread Nile delta, and Succoth as the modern
Tell el-Maskhutah, then the first leg of the escape route carried
the Israelites about 32 miles in a southern and slightly eastern
direction, through their own Goshen district (Gen. 47:27; Exod.
8:22; 9:26). Their next camp is at "Etham, on the edge of the
wilderness" (Exod. 13:20). But now they are told to "turn back
and encamp in front of Pi-ha-hiroth, between Migdol and the
sea, in front of Baal-zephon; you shall encamp over against it, by
the sea" (14:2). If they actually turned back, then they pro-
ceeded north again and obviously encamped adjacent to a body
of water, which could have been Timsah or, if this turning back
extended sufficiently far to the north, Menzaleh. But Etham (nowhere else mentioned) and Pi-ha-hiroth and Migdol (both named
in Egyptian records) all remain unidentified. Baal-zephon is
known to be the name of a Canaanite deity to whom a temple
once stood in Tahpanhes, to which city Jeremiah was taken in
the sixth century (Jer. 43:1-7). Does Baal-zephon, then, mean
Tahpanhes, the modern Tell Defneh? If so, the backward leg
brought them again to a point only about twenty miles southeast
of their original place of departure, Ra-amses, on the southern
extremities of Lake Menzaleh. This may indeed be the route of
march, but it remains a reconstruction less than decisive.

In this first section (13:17—14:4) of the complete story of
the escape (13:17—15:21) we note another item of interest.
Joseph's foreknowledge of this event was introduced first in
Genesis 50:25. The dying Joseph extracted the solemn promise
from his survivors (binding, of course, on all subsequent generations until fulfilled) that his remains would go out of Egypt with
Israel. This obligation was now discharged (13:19). It is not at
all improbable that the bones of Joseph, the father of the tribes

of Ephraim and Manasseh (see Gen. 48:3-6), went along with members of these two intimately related clans.

In the second portion of the narrative of this episode (14:5-20) Egypt pursues, and the critical scene is set. It has already been pointed out that, as Egypt understood her own affairs, the Exodus, since it is not mentioned in Egyptian records, must have been regarded as a minor crisis, representing a relatively inconsequential loss. The narrative itself testifies that with the Hebrews there went up also "a mixed multitude" (Exod. 12:38), that is, a conglomerate lot, hangers-on to Egypt's productive life and land, some of whom no doubt were as much a liability as an asset. That these escapees were nevertheless pursued by the Egyptians with the firm intent to force them back into Egypt's servitude again we do not for a moment question; and that it was *in Israel's eyes* a matter of such moment as to require the personal leadership of the king himself we are certain. But that Rameses II, known also as Rameses the Great (or for that matter any other Pharaoh of the Nineteenth or Eighteenth Dynasty), put himself at the head of his entire complement of chariotry (14:6-7, 9) in execution of such a task without leaving in any Egyptian records an account of such an event seems to many interpreters improbable.

More important in the narrative is the fact that in the midst of this highly tentative, terrifying, panic-prone venture of faith, the loud wail of unfaith is sounded. Our freedom to serve God (so they reasoned) is only a dim possibility; the continued pursuit of that freedom means the irrevocable renunciation of all the aspects of security we have ever known. We cannot face the quest of freedom in God's service even for God's sake when, in the course of the quest, we are propelled into an existence that is a vacuum, devoid of all the symbols of security—ground to walk on, means of subsistence, and some reasonable assurance of continuity. Let us go back to Egypt. Let us return to life and meaning tangibly supported by human means and human devices—even though they be Egyptian!

It is a fundamental cry, this wail of unfaith. And no man may sit in judgment on it, since every man's life of faith is tormented by the same essential cry. This is precisely why this narrative of the Exodus and the wandering in the wilderness and the entrance into Canaan claims the attention of succeeding generations of those who, in varying kind and degree, espouse the life of faith.

This is the story of every man's tentative, terrifying, panic-prone venture of faith!

The cry is thematic, which is simply to say that it recurs, like the theme of a musical composition, to give characteristic form and emphasis to the whole. Substantially the same cry can be observed with colorful variation in 16:3; 17:3; Numbers 14:3; 20:3-4; 21:5. Again the same cry can be heard from the rebels, Dathan and Abiram, with a vicious inversion of the Word's promise through Moses—the bitterest kind of repudiation of the whole venture of leaving the security of Egypt for the seeming insecurity of the service of the Lord in a new land purported to be "flowing with milk and honey" (Num. 16:12-14). At any rate, the basic cry represented here is one known in essence to us all: Better to serve Egypt than die in this wilderness; better to be slave and idolater than proceed on the insecure and insubstantial ground of faith!

Exodus gives a prominent variation on this central biblical theme. The choice is on the one hand a land that is always in some sense a land of promise, always in some sense distant, remote; or on the other, return to Egypt! And Egypt is always there. We *were* Pharaoh's slaves. God *did* bring us out. We *are* Pharaoh's slaves. God *does* bring us out. But it is our act too. It is not only God who acts, but we who act, in unfaith, in rebellion, in panic.

"The LORD brought us out of Egypt with a mighty hand . . ." (Deut. 6:21). Yes. But we made it exceedingly difficult for him, and the nature of the bringing out is shaped as well by his action as by our responses, faithful and unfaithful, and his inescapably consequent *re*-action. If we are brought out, at what cost to him are we brought out?

This is the story of God and man in interaction. It is the (humanly) unpredictable and always complex interplay of Word and word.

Now Moses speaks high, strong words, but not in rebuke; this cry of unfaith is met with reassurance (14:13). The following verse, however, may not be interpreted as encouragement to take a rest since the Lord is about to take care of everything himself. In this short verse (only five words in Hebrew) is the real rebuke, following the word of reassurance. The sense is this: Hold your tongues! The Lord fights for us! So, in appropriate narrative motion, there follows the word to Moses: "Tell the people of Israel

to go forward" (vs. 15). This is the Word probing for the positive human response, effecting God's purpose in interaction with
the word, with the performance, with the faith and unfaith of
man.

Verses 17-18, like the old confession of faith in Deuteronomy
6:21-23, idealize the Exodus event for the primary purpose of
praising God, stressing the two opposing components, the glory
of the Lord and the glory of Pharaoh-Egypt. And the great episode of the actual crossing of the Sea is finally broached, in verses
19-20, with the description of the relative positions of the two
camps, Israel and Egypt, as the pillar of cloud and darkness
hides each from the other.

The third stage of the narrative concerns the dramatic crossing
(14:21-31). With eyes and mind trained and conditioned as ours
are, we cannot read this section without some consciousness of
the process whereby there are now merged in one account originally independent motifs which are not entirely compatible in
combination. In the following parallel accounts we do not de-
ceive ourselves with the assurance that we have accurately dis-
entangled two originally separate strata of tradition. If we call
one "the J stratum" and the other "the P stratum" we do so (as
always in this discussion) without dogmatic inferences as to
sources, scope, form, and date of the arrangement, or composition, or integration, or entity of such strata. We mean only to
accent the multiform quality of the final product, and to suggest
that earlier and later collections of tradition reproduce "memories" differing in detail but always remarkably unified in what is
essentially proclaimed, in what is in faith affirmed as to enduring sense and meaning.

(21b) . . . and the LORD drove the sea back by a strong east wind all night, and made the sea dry land . . .	(21a, c) Then Moses stretched out his hand over the sea . . . and the waters were divided.
(24) And in the morning watch the LORD . . . looked down upon the host of the Egyptians . . .	(22) And the people of Israel went into the midst of the sea on dry ground, the waters be-ing a wall to them on their right hand and on their left.
(25) clogging [or binding— perhaps, caused to bog down] their chariot wheels so that	(23) The Egyptians pursued, and went in after them into the midst of the sea, all Phar-

they drove heavily; and the Egyptians said, "Let us flee from before Israel; for the LORD fights for them against the Egyptians."

(27b) . . . and the sea returned to its wonted flow [the inference is clear: the wind abated and the water returned to its customary level] when the morning appeared . . . and the LORD routed the Egyptians in the midst of the sea.

aoh's horses, his chariots, and his horsemen.

(26) Then the LORD said to Moses, "Stretch out your hand over the sea, that the water may come back upon the Egyptians . . ."

(27a) So Moses stretched forth his hand over the sea . . .

(28a) The waters returned and covered the chariots and the horsemen and all the host of Pharaoh . . .

The first account represents the event as crucially conditioned by "natural" phenomena—an abnormally low tide produced by uncommonly strong winds; the returning of the water; the rendering ineffective of the Egyptian chariots by the now miry shallows; and the necessary abandonment of the chase. The other account represents a memory more impressed with what we would term the quality of the miraculous. It is important, however, to acknowledge the fact that both interpretations affirm with equal insistence the decisive role of God. Essentially the same two differing interpretations are to be seen combined in the present account of the plagues. It is further to be noted that this motif of the phenomenally dry crossing also appears in the narrative of Israel's entrance into Canaan (Joshua 3:13; see also II Kings 2:8).

In one form or the other, or in some earlier combination of two or more such forms, Israel rehearsed, retold, re-enacted, and relived this most significant single moment of her past. We ought to understand, of any such incomprehensible moment of time, that the participants themselves would be unable to answer the question, "Exactly what happened?" The pursued were an ill-organized, virtually unarmed, and now panic-ridden column of walking men, women, children, flocks, bearing such conglomerate and awkward possessions as could not or would not be left behind. The pursuers, in whatever numbers, were a compact, disciplined, swiftly maneuverable unit, equipped with the world's finest weapons and faced now only with the relatively easy assignment of turning back this clumsy herd of helpless fugitives. How

many in the Moses group, facing such odds, anticipated any
better outcome than frustration, return to Egypt, and the imposition of brutally punitive measures? How many indeed feared
death, or worse, at the hands of Pharaoh's lusty charioteers, now
fast closing the gap between pursuer and pursued?

The item which is clearly incontrovertible is that suddenly the
pursued found themselves without pursuer. The chase was a
chase no more. The hunter had abandoned the hunt. We would
assume that this impossible piece of news passed from the rear
of the pathetically slow, ragged, fleeing column toward the front,
moved along on incredulous voices, pushed ahead from group to
group, from section to section, deeply doubted but ecstatically
supported by hope suddenly reborn. Can this be? In the name of
the Lord and by his Word, is this possible? Can the convicted be
reprieved? Can the lost be found? Can the dead be alive? And when
the incredible fact, now no less incredible, becomes confirmed,
forcing acknowledgment from those who but a moment ago
knew themselves to be convicted, lost, and dying—what then?

The traumatic act of realization surely removed the precise
details of this unbelievable outcome quite beyond exact recall,
even by the immediate participants, to say nothing of all the subsequent generations of sympathetic participants repeating the
line of re-enactment: "*We* were Pharaoh's slaves in Egypt; and
the LORD brought *us* out" (Deut. 6:21), or "The Egyptians
treated *us* harshly . . . Then *we* cried to the LORD . . . and the
LORD brought *us* out" (Deut. 26:6-8). And all continuing accounts, reflecting the common faith of those actually involved as
well as of the countless multitude of sympathetic participants in
the ensuing centuries, agree that this was then, and is now, an
occasion of praise to God. Deliverance from Egypt, in original
fact or in symbolic rehearsal (see Isaiah 43:1-2), is God's deliverance; it is the work of his Word through Moses, or the prophets—or Christ.

The present, final account of this marvelous episode of Israel's
redemption at the Sea is firm and unambiguous as to its climax.
These bitterly suppressed people in their ragged procession, remembering now the word of Moses conveying the Word of Another, in overwhelming realization that only this Word could
effect so glorious and impossible an outcome; this company of
the lost, the enslaved, the dying, now found and freed and given
life by God; this weak, diffuse body of humanity suddenly made

almost terrifyingly aware of its unity and entity as created out of God's unfathomable purpose—these people in this company, in this body, all break forth into a spontaneous hymn of praise, more shout than song, more chant than anthem, more cry of ecstasy than conscious composition:

> "Sing to the LORD, for he has triumphed
>   gloriously;
> the horse and his rider he has thrown
>   into the sea" (15:21; see 15:1).

This, the song of Moses and Miriam, comprises the fourth section of the narrative here. Certain specific questions arise in the study of this section which, in our judgment, cannot be unequivocally answered. No considerable measure of agreement has been reached concerning (1) the date, even approximate, of the composition of the long hymn in 15:1-18; (2) the possible original function of this hymn; or (3) the relationships of this hymn to the shorter "Song of Miriam" in verse 21, and to the preceding prose narrative of the marvelous escape.

Commonly the two lines attributed to Miriam in verse 21 are thought to be exceedingly old. There is indeed no good reason to doubt their origin (in approximately if not precisely this same form) in the very historical episode itself; nor is Miriam's role as in some sense leader and conductor of the spontaneous demonstration in any way implausible (compare, for example, the Song of Deborah in Judges 5).

It is further probable that the longer song, attributed to Moses (see also Deuteronomy 32-33 and Psalm 90), is an expansion of the original, authentic two lines. It has occasionally been argued that the reverse is true, that the short form represents the title or condensed summary of the original longer poem.

While it is impossible to say precisely for what purpose this hymn was *created*, we see no reason to doubt that it *served* from the beginning of its existence a function in the formal rhythm of the Israelite religious year. We suggest, then—though still holding that specific, dogmatic answers are impossible—that the poem in substantially its present form came into existence within a century or so of the event of the Exodus; in repeated, annual liturgical use it probably became relatively "fixed"; and probably it was appropriately modified, possibly chiefly in interpretation, when the cultic rehearsal of God's creation of Israel was shifted to Jerusalem.

What of the relationship between the long poem and the preceding prose narrative? If one is in some significant sense dependent upon the other, priority lies with the poem. It is indeed, we suspect, the epic quality of the poem, its magnificent "license," its very *poetic* form, which are responsible for the "J" and "P" readings so troublesome to the modern interpreter. The fact is that the same epic quality, the same kind of license, and indeed the same essential poetic character permeate the prose—but the form remains prose.

The fact is, of course, that whether by wind and tide, or by giant walls of water which formed between a dry pathway through the midst of the sea, what is affirmed is the Lord's Power over all power—human power as represented by Pharaoh's host, and natural power as represented by the wind and waves (see Matt. 8:23-27; Mark 4:35-41; Luke 8:22-25).

Here, then, is the story of Israel's coming out of Egypt. It is the account of a people's birth-hour. It is the emphatic declaration that Israel did not simply happen, but was created. It is a narrative dominated by the tenacious struggles of Moses versus Pharaoh, of meaning versus chaos, even of life versus death. But the story is so accented as to affirm a faith, to proclaim a conviction: this is creation by God and his Word-through-Moses—but brought to fulfillment by the response in faith of Moses and even of Israel. It is a mighty act of God in, through, and out of a mighty act of faith sufficient to override the brash, persistent, painful, sometimes uncontrollable, bursts of mortal unfaith.

It is a story of God and man, Word and word, in interaction.

Israel and the Wilderness; Moses and the Lord
(15:22—17:16)

What Shall We Drink? (15:22-27)

The location and limits of the wilderness of Shur, into which Moses now leads Israel from the Reed Sea (vs. 22), can be only very roughly approximated (see Gen. 16:7; 20:1; 25:18; in Num. 33:8 it is called the wilderness of Etham). Obviously it borders on Egypt, but any more exact definition depends on the still problematical reconstruction of the geography of the Exodus-Sinai events. Israel is, in any case, now east of Egypt, and is penetrating the Sinai peninsula. Three days' journey for such a company would, we suspect, hardly exceed forty miles.

In historical times water has always been a relatively rare and precious commodity in this area; and thirst has been and will always be a torment. In a full generation of movement through these arid wastelands, the protest from Israel's thirsty throats must have been voiced repeatedly. We will encounter it again at 17:1-7 (see also Num. 20:1-12).

It is a pattern which becomes familiar now: Israel complains to Moses; Moses complains to the Lord; and the Lord, usually in communication with Moses, effects the situation's remedy or redemption. And this is, of course, the theme which the narrative is concerned to emphasize. That Israel survived at all and was given ultimately to enter the Land of Canaan was due to God, and his effective Word to Moses. Thus faith was always reaffirmed after the act of unfaith, and the relationship was restored by which alone Israel was created and sustained. It is not strange, then, that the narrative, concentrating on the theme of the relationship between Israel and the Lord, pays relatively slight attention to such "practical" matters as route of march, identification of places, and even sequence of episodes. The important matter is that the account give primary and emphatic expression to the interpretation of faith—to the sure belief that this epoch in Israel's life, no less than the moment of coming out of Egypt, owed its successful outcome to, and found its meaning in, the relationship of God and people.

What shall we drink? Here is an oasis (a well, or a spring, or a pool?); here is water, and we are desperately thirsty. But this stuff is undrinkable, bitter! How right that the place is named Marah, "Bitterness"! And how bitter now our life and lot!

Again, as is the case with other wonders attendant upon Israel's life, one *may* rationalize: certain unpalatable waters can be and have been "healed" by the introduction of neutralizing or sweetening barks. Moses, a man of long experience in wilderness survival, had learned in Midian the formula for sweetening bitter water, and applied it now.

Such may indeed have been the case. But in any event, it is in violation of the nature and character of the tradition (and, we suspect, of the faith of Moses himself and the people under his leadership) to isolate the instance and reduce it *in meaning* to a case of primitive but effective chemistry. This is one of a vast series of wonders, almost any one of which may be so "reduced," occurring to a people whose creation and survival are effected against seemingly impossible odds. This is only one wonder in inseparable sequence with a progression of wonders, experienced by this people. Then, as later, they remained unutterably convinced that every wonder seen thus as part of the great over-all wonder of a people's marvelous creation was God's purposive response both to the faith and to the unfaith of Israel. To regard it as possible and even probable that Moses had had previous experience in the rudimentary wilderness art of healing bitter waters is an interpretation which in no sense violates the narrative's sense of faith, *provided* that the "hand" or Word of the Lord, and the Lord's intention and purpose, are seen in the earlier "showing" (vs. 25) of the healing tree, that is, if the *meaning* of Moses' whole life is seen in the divine intent to create a People of God who will serve in history the purposes of God.

Is this healing tree, cast by divine direction into the bitter waters, in any legitimate sense at all a "foreshadowing" of the crucifixion "tree" which God's redemptive love threw into the world for the healing of all the bitterness of human existence? In one sense, of course, emphatically not: ancient Israel certainly did not incorporate this story, voluntarily or involuntarily, in miraculous foreknowledge of the crucified Jesus. On the other hand, the essential faith which is enshrined in this story *is* the forerunner of the faith which in the Gospels so persistently cast Jesus Christ in the role of healer of all kinds of bitterness, the faith which appropriates to the suffering of the Cross the line first spoken of the Servant of the Lord: "with his stripes we are healed" (Isa. 53:5; see also I Peter 2:24).

In 15:25b-26, the framework of the narrative is showing. This is the language, the vocabulary, and the style of the Book of Deuteronomy and of the "school" of editors in that particular stratum. In this perspective, the aspect of healing recalls Egypt's suffering under the plagues; this leads to the characteristic Deuteronomic advice that Israel's well-being lies in observance of the Lord's "statute . . . ordinance . . . commandments." Here the enduring theological meaning of the little episode is succinctly stated, testifying to the remarkable measure of inspiration in the present form of multiple intertwined strata: "I am the LORD, your healer."

So the Israelites came to Elim, described with charm—and not at all irrelevantly, for this is, after Marah, a lush oasis—as boasting twelve springs and seventy palm trees (vs. 27).

What Shall We Eat? (16:1-36)

We know no more about the location and area of the wilderness of Sin than we do of the wilderness of Shur. It may be that Sin derives its name from Sinai and that it was located, therefore, at or around the base of the sacred mountain. Geographical problems remain, and we must be content to leave such questions open. We can actually visualize three possible routes across the Sinai peninsula—the northern route proceeding east (via Sirbonis) and then southeast; another following out of Egypt a generally easterly direction through, roughly, the central part of the Sinaitic triangle; and a third route taking the Israelites in a southeasterly march toward the lower point of the peninsula and the traditional location of Mount Sinai.

The Israelites drank their fill at Elim with its twelve springs (one for each tribe, although the pattern of twelve tribes was hardly then apparent) and its seventy palm trees (one for each of the elders of Israel, not yet appointed). Thirst has given way to hunger. So again—and this, too, happened more than once in the span of several decades of wilderness residence (see Num. 11)—the cry of complaint ("murmurings") is heard in the camp, and bitter it is (16:3). Would that we had died full in Egypt rather than die empty here, by slow starvation!

The present form of the entire chapter shows a number of signs of Priestly editing, that is, of having been considerably reworked by the Priestly historians. One observes Aaron's role as Moses' co-captain, a strong interest in the institution of the Sabbath, certain characteristic words (for example, "congregation"), and the effort to chronologize (16:1). But at the same time, the narrative still bears the marks of its character prior to such editing, and we therefore reject any notion that this is a late creation of unrestrained popular imagination.

The story retains some solid contact with the time and the people, some historical recollection of the epoch, although the episodes represented may originally have been separated both geographically and in time. The reference to "manna" in Num-

bers 11:4-9 as "bdellium" is a clue. The word means a fragrant
gum; and this strongly supports the identification of manna with
a sweet substance which is found adhering to the tamarisk tree,
a honey-like sap sucked out by insects and available in greatest
quantity in June.

Quail in large numbers annually migrate from Europe in the
fall, September and October, crossing in flight the Mediterranean
Sea to fall in exhaustion along the Sinai coast. If the Reed Sea
was not Sirbonis, Israel nevertheless must at some time have fre-
quented the coastal area of Sinai; perhaps on more than one occasion they found quail ready prey for snaring by hand. And
with the return of spring each year, the nomadic wanderers invaded the groves of the tamarisk to pull off and eat in quantity
the sweet bdellium. The memory of such events is here preserved
together with what must also have been the faith of those who
ate the quail and the manna: We were hungry, and the Lord fed
us!

The suggestion that quail and manna recall different phenomena, encountered at different times of the year and in different
places, raises again the question of order and sequence of events.
It is unlikely that both of these happened en route to Mount
Sinai. It may be, in fact, that the episodes recorded here in Exodus
as having taken place between the departure from Egypt and
the arrival at Sinai occurred for the most part after Sinai, in the
sustained decades of semi-nomadism prior to the invasion of
Canaan. Such a sequence is indeed presupposed in Numbers,
where duplicates, parallels, or repetitions of some of these inci-
dents are narrated in a post-Sinai sequence.

The daily diet of manna was considerable: an omer (approximately two quarts) per day per person (vs. 16). No merely natural explanation of the phenomenon is presupposed in the narrative, for, regardless of the amount gathered, each person found
himself with exactly the amount needed for his own sustenance
(see Paul's application of this remarkable observance in II Corinthians 8:15).

It is further apparent that the story is told in such a way as
to lend the strongest support to the institution of the Sabbath,
the seventh day of rest. Here the Sabbath is seen as already in
practice in Israel's earliest days as a people. And in fact some
form of Sabbath observance is not impossible. The present account, however, is colored by later development of the institution

in Israel and testifies to its fundamental importance (as does the
Creation account of Genesis 1-2).

Finally, the conclusion of chapter 16 in verses 31-36 recalls
that the experience of the provision of food in the otherwise
barren wilderness was tangibly memorialized; that a jar full of
manna (or something symbolizing manna?) was placed and kept
before the "testimony" which is the Ark of the Covenant (see
the comment on ch. 25). Israel is to remember throughout her
generations the grace of the Lord by which she was marvelously
nurtured. Let her be reminded of this so that she may discern-
ingly comprehend not simply what she was but, because of what
she was, what she *is,* holding life *now* by virtue of God's sustaining grace. Let her be reminded of this by the presence of a mute
object, a simple jar, standing before Israel's holiest and most
treasured symbol, the Ark. Let her be reminded of this in every
span of seven days by trusting still in God's provident grace, and
undertaking on each seventh day absolutely none of the regular
duties for the preservation and maintenance of life.

Is the Lord Among Us or Not? (17:1-7)

Israel proceeds "by stages" according to "the mouth of the
Lord" (so literally for "the commandment of the Lord"); that is,
her movements through the wilderness are at the Word's direction. The location of Rephidim has not been identified; this place-
name therefore does not help us in determining the whereabouts
of Israel and the sacred mountain ("Horeb," vs. 6). Water is in
insufficient supply (see 15:22-27; Num. 20:1-13), and Moses
rightly interprets the complaint of the people as a challenge not
only to his own leadership but to God's as well (vs. 2). In fear
for his very life (vs. 4), Moses turns to the Lord.

The Lord's presence at a designated rock produces water when
Moses strikes the rock with his rod, an episode again more
colorfully and violently described in Numbers 20; and the spot,
according to the tradition, acquires not one but two symbolic
names, Massah ("Proof"—"Why do you put the Lord to the
proof?" vs. 2) and Meribah ("Contention"—"Why do you find
fault [contend] with me?" vs. 2). In Numbers 20 the same kind
of episode also accounts for the place-name, Meribah; but there
it is associated not with Massah but with Kadesh ("Sanctified"—
"the Lord . . . showed himself holy among them," Num. 20:1,
13). Massah and Meribah come later to have a figurative use in

the biblical language, denoting rejection of the way and possibilities of faith (Deut. 6:16; 9:22; 33:8; Ps. 95:8).

For the rest, we can only suggest that thirst must often have been a critical problem in the wilderness years; that names of people and places were subjects of acute interest because the name was deemed to be appropriate *in meaning* to the object named; that Israel may, therefore, on occasion have renamed a site (or, by a greater or lesser modification in sound, given the old name a new, Hebrew meaning) significant for her own experience there; and that Massah and Meribah represent the merging of two similar stories.

The theme is, of course, always the primary concern: "Is the LORD among us or not?" The popular perversion of the religion of the worship of the Lord in Israel, like "popular Christianity," betrayed a readiness, even an eagerness, to invert the true relationship, "We are his," to read instead, "He is ours!" It was thought (how wrongly!) that it was God's business to see to it that his people were rendered marvelously immune to the hazards of existence, time, accident, and environment. In the same way, when we find ourselves prey to that which is in fact an inevitable, plaguing accompaniment of existence, we are prone to say as Israel is remembered to have said, "The Lord has deserted us!"

It was and it is, to be sure, a problem of faith to affirm that God is among us even in adverse circumstances, when our relationship to him appears to be nothing more (but what authority, indeed, have we for demanding more than this?) than servant, even Suffering Servant, and when there is no rational, tangible demonstration that we are his. Jesus condemned us all, both those before him and those after him, when he repudiated the sign-seekers (Matt. 12:39; Mark 8:12; Luke 11:29). There are those who are eager to substitute the formula of magic which, properly executed, guarantees the magic-maker's glory, for the formula of faith which, in the last analysis, guarantees only God's glory and the forgiveness and *ultimate* healing of all our woe and bitterness.

When the Word says, "I will be with you, on *my* terms," our word responds, "Be with me on *my* terms!" So there is recalled the bitter, sarcastic cry of Israel, always ready on the lips at the first sign of adversity, "Is the LORD among us or not?" There is also recalled a marvelously tolerant and patient word of the Lord which repeatedly in effect provides the "sign" and offers tangible reassurance—although, be it noted, in matters by and large of sheer survival. In any case the thematic cry from Israel's unfaith, "Is the LORD among us or not?" is answered with a resounding, "Yes."

Write This As a Memorial (17:8-16)

"Write this . . . and recite it" (vs. 14) refers specifically to Israel's victory over a hostile people, the Amalekites. But this is the final and climactic episode in a series of four (15:22—17: 16). Apparently these four episodes are put in sequence as variations on the theme that this is Israel's glorious hour only as it is God's glorious hour; that the word of Israel (that is, her overt, apparent nature and function as a people) becomes established against insuperable odds by the Word of the Lord (God's communicated or revealed nature and power and purpose) in mutually responsive interaction. This is illustrated in the initial period in the wilderness by three episodes having to do with the first fundamental necessity of survival, food and drink, and a fourth episode dealing with the second basic threat to existence, attack from hostile forces. The section then affirms the Word-word conquest of hunger and thirst and war—although in human existence these continue to be the most prevalent and dreaded agents of death. It is surely *total* conquest which is thus recited and memorialized and believed in faith.

Specifically, it should be repeated, it is the threat of annihilation at the hands of Amalek that is celebrated in this episode. The Amalekites were distantly related to Israel; they are descendants of Esau, Jacob's brother (Gen. 36:12). Their center of activity appears to have been in the Kadesh area, as was Israel's through much of her sojourn in the wilderness (see Num. 13:29; 14:25). We encounter them repeatedly in bitter conflict with Israel in the following centuries (Num. 14:43-45; Judges 3:13; 6:3, 33; I Sam. 15), until their virtual annihilation, apparently, at the hands of David (I Sam. 30). They appear only once again thereafter (I Chron. 4:41-43).

It may be, although it is nowhere so stated, that Amalek and Israel fought for possession of Kadesh. This early encounter is recalled as an uneven contest; obviously Israel is no match for Amalek, man for man, weapon for weapon. The narrative presents problems of several kinds. It is not in itself among the more refined stories of the Bible. It reflects an intensely bitter hatred

for the Amalekites, a human kind of hatred which is imputed to
God (17:14), so that it is the very Word which speaks the fierce
judgment of annihilation upon Amalek. Moses is reduced to
somewhat unflattering stature in an action, interestingly enough,
that is not authorized by the Word. It is not until verse 14 that
the Lord enters the scene, and then with lines which seem out of
true character—although beyond any doubt accurately representing the popular attribution of intensely localized and limited perspectives to God. Joshua appears here too early in the story: he
is introduced in 33:11 as a young man, and that is much later
(see 24:13; 32:17; Num. 11:28). And Moses, whose great work
is only just beginning, is apparently near the close of his life, for
inferentially, his physical powers are waning. To all this one
might add that the text itself is at points in dubious state of preservation, so that one may only *conjecture* (see the marginal note
for verse 16) as to the original sense.

Now this is not for a moment to impugn the value of the story
both historically and theologically. On the contrary. On the one
hand this representation both of Moses and of God reflects very
ancient times. If we cannot ourselves accept this characterization
of the Word as final, we are nevertheless confident that the true
word of Israel is here spoken! It may be that the story was originally preserved because it imparted to the rallying ground of Kadesh the kind of sacred authority implied in Moses' building an
altar there (vss. 15-16). As it stands now, however, it forms the
climax and summary of a section constructed so as to illustrate
simply and effectively God's conquest of the fundamental threats
to Israel's existence in her first independently drawn breaths, immediately following her hazardous birth out of Egypt. By the
process of an exceedingly trying Word-word response and interaction, Israel survived an improbable birth and the first critically
threatened days of her new existence.

Moses and Jethro (18:1-27)

Now the narrative turns, as Israel also in time must have
turned, to the crucial matter of consolidation and organization.
Moses' years in Midian, already implicitly recalled more than
once as decisively effecting the successful resolution of crisis, now
again constructively qualify the nature of events. This time the

matter concerns the very person of Jethro, Moses' father-in-law (see also Num. 10:29-36).

Reunion (18:1-12)

The scene is brief, clear, and, in itself, uncomplicated. Jethro brings Zipporah, Moses' wife, and their two sons, whom Moses had apparently sent back to Midian before the exodus from Egypt, and the family is reunited. Moses himself reports to Jethro on all that has taken place since their separation. The reunion is then celebrated with a sacrifice and a common meal to which Aaron and the "elders of Israel" are invited.

The incident takes place at the "mountain of God." Wherever they are, and wherever the sacred mountain, the distance between Moses and his family has been closing as Israel has moved in an easterly direction across the Sinai peninsula. Jethro, his daughter, and his grandsons may not have traveled very far.

Even the casual reader of Exodus must find himself occasionally speculating about the real relationship between Moses and Jethro. Jethro is a priest. We are nowhere informed about the deity to whose service as priest he is consecrated. But Moses, while living as a favored son-in-law in the home of Jethro, is confronted and the course of his life radically changed by "Yahweh," a name previously unknown to Moses but referring in very meaning to the One God. Now reunited with Moses, this same priest offers "a burnt offering and sacrifices" (vs. 12) to the same Lord who has just wrought Israel's deliverance.

Was Jethro then a priest of the Lord? The oldest stratum of the tradition (J) consistently represents the Lord as having been worshiped without interruption from time immemorial among the southern tribes of Judah and her relations, such as the Kenites, the Calebites, the Othnielites (see Judges 1). Jethro was a Midianite, and more particularly a Kenite, that is, a member of a sub-clan of the larger tribe of Midian (Judges 4:11—"Hobab" is a third name, along with Reuel, in Exodus 2:18, and Jethro, for Moses' father-in-law). He is in fact called specifically "the Kenite" in Judges 1:16, where also his descendants are seen in close association with the tribe of Judah. Was the scope of God's revelation to Moses effected in part through the agency of Jethro, priest in Midian? The question can and must be asked. It cannot be decisively answered. The view of Moses' possible indebtedness, in these terms, to Jethro has been proposed with many variations for about a century, but it remains only hypothesis.

Lesson in Administration (18:13-27)

Whether or not the *religion* of Moses in form or content was directly indebted to the religion of Jethro, there can be little doubt that Jethro gave Moses significant advice in matters of civil administration. Although the advice comes from Jethro, it is implicitly the commandment of God (vss. 23-24). The number of administrators chosen is not indicated here (in the similar passage in Numbers 11:16 it is the potent number 70).

Approximately what size group of wandering Israelites, then, are we justified in visualizing? In these pages we have throughout assumed a relatively small company—a few thousand. But even with a total company of several thousand, Moses was attempting the impossible in personally administering all matters, ecclesiastical, civil, and juridical. Jethro's counsel was wisely given and wisely heeded.

So Jethro takes his leave of Moses (18:27), we assume with some satisfaction in what he has been able to effect. The parallel narrative in Numbers 10:29-32 records Moses' urging his father-in-law to stay with them, agreeing in any case in the very positive estimate of Jethro and his relationship to Moses and Israel.

The tradition as recorded in Exodus turns now, with an epoch completed, to a body of material with the sacred mountain as its nucleus. The act of Israel's creation-deliverance, offering initially a miserable prognosis and fulfilled against unbelievable odds, is rounded out with the establishment of some order and stability in the necessarily improvised and inevitably confused structure of Israel's new existence as a people. God and God's Word through Moses have effected the impossible—deliverance from Egypt, salvation in the dire threat of extinction by thirst, famine, and sword, and now a workable administrative structure adequate to the immediate needs of a group increasingly involved in the complex, self-conscious problems of a new people, with a new freedom, with a new and uneasy responsibility.

THE MAKING AND MEANING OF COVENANT
Exodus 19:1—24:18

This section of six chapters is in its present form and position in the Old Testament the introductory unit to a tremendous block of material extending through the remainder of the Book of Exodus to embrace all of Leviticus and the first part of Numbers, terminating with Numbers 10:10. This unit, Exodus 19:1—Numbers 10:10, is an editorial creation, comprising varied traditional materials brought together from a broad span of centuries, and provided with integrity as a unit in the *place*, Sinai. This giant block of material appears to have been inserted in the midst of a section unified in the place, Kadesh, for Kadesh appears as the area of operations both before and after the extended material centered at Sinai. Kadesh is not, to be sure, mentioned by name in Exodus 16-18, but parallels to these stories in Numbers (especially Numbers 11 and 20) clearly belong to the Kadesh cycle, toward which center Israel moves directly from Sinai (Num. 10: 11—13:26); and it is highly probable that the contest with Amalek (Exod. 17:8-13) as well as the meeting with Jethro (Exod. 18; Num. 10:29-32) took place in the vicinity of Kadesh.

Most of this material centered at Sinai shows signs of long association with priestly circles; that is, it owes its preservation if not necessarily its origin to this increasingly influential element in the life of the Old Testament people. But it also contains a significant nucleus which is distinctly not of priestly cast, although certainly incorporated with the approval and by the design of the priestly perspective. We may term this material "Yahwistic," or even prophetic if we push back, as we must, the limits of essential prophetism to the tenth century, and possibly earlier. This material largely comprises Exodus 19-24, the six chapters now before us, and Exodus 32-34; and within this core, Exodus 19, 20, and 24 appear to have provided the basic framework for the unit. The initial structure was simple and theologically eloquent: The glory, the presence, of the Lord is revealed with uncommonly convincing power—the term which is often used for this kind of revelation is "theophany"—signifying the Lord's commitment to the Covenant (a pact, an agreement, a working arrangement between two parties) implicit in the divine-human encounter (ch. 19). The senior party to the Covenant, the Lord, having already committed himself, and having revealed his glory, now makes known his will—the Ten Commandments—for the other Covenant party, Israel (ch. 20). In chapter 24, Israel's acceptance of and commitment to this Covenant with its fundamental responsibilities is symbolized and celebrated in a cultic act which includes the shedding of blood and a communion meal, both signifying the absolutely irrevocable quality of the commitment.

It is surely unnecessary to point out that this same essential theological pattern reappears, this time centering in the person of Christ, in the New Testament which is the New Covenant. The glory of God is revealed, his Word is given, uniquely (such is the Christian affirmation) in Christ, signifying God's commitment to that Covenant in which he offers to redeem man from all his multiform, perennial Egypts, and bring him into the freedom of his service, to take him for his own. He then makes known his will, in the person and gospel of Christ. Christian acceptance of and commitment to this Covenant is symbolized in faith's appropriation of Christ's death, and its continued celebration and reappropriation in the Holy Communion.

As has so often been the case in preceding episodes in Exodus, here too we must be cautious in moving from the articulation of the event to the actual historical form, sequence, content, and significance of the episode. We have no doubt that, in substantially the simple form just described, the making and meaning of the Sinai Covenant was from early times re-enacted in a kind of liturgical celebration. There is no reason to doubt a firm relationship between the early form of the celebration and the structure of the historical occasion giving rise to it. One sees little ground for denying that Moses did return with Israel to the scene of his first encounter with the Word and Presence of the Lord—an encounter utterly transforming his and Israel's existence; that *the* Covenant between the Lord and Israel was here, in precisely such simple, moving terms, solemnly attested by both parties; and that the first pre-Christian biblical celebration of Holy Communion actually occurred in conjunction with the sealing of Covenant.

But in its final form the Sinai tradition is obviously vastly expanded, leaving with the reader the impression that virtually the total structure of thoroughly formalized and institutionalized religion came into full-blown existence at Sinai. The process of augmentation is already apparent in what we have termed the nucleus in chapters 19, 20, and 24. The Ten Commandments themselves (in Hebrew, literally, "ten words") are certainly not now in their earliest form; and there is some reason to suspect not only expansion and even modification, but the substitution of another "edition," so to speak, for what was originally there, although it is to be remarked that, if so, little difference existed between the two editions. To this probable nucleus of the three chapters, the long section of instructional material, chapters 21-23, was added, as was the material in 32-34; and in the centuries following, there were incorporated other materials relevant to the character of the Sinai event.

Here we are immediately concerned only with that section in Exodus (chs. 19-24) which constitutes the introduction to the whole body of material associated with Sinai and which contains the original nucleus around which the whole complex ultimately formed.

The Glory of the Lord at Sinai (19:1-25)

The word "theophany" is compounded of the Greek word meaning "God" and the verb "to appear." There is nothing objectionable in referring to chapter 19 as a "theophany" *if* it is understood to mean a manifestation of God. But it is crucially important to observe that the narrative makes no claim that the Lord himself, the very Person of God, *the* Deity, here made his visible appearance.

The Initiating Word (19:1-9a)

One notable feature of the introductory scene is the prominence of words having to do not with vision but with audition. Four such words occur in verse 3 alone: "The LORD *called . . . saying*, 'Thus you shall *say* . . . and *tell* . . .' " With reference to the past, the passage continues in the next verse, "You have *seen* what I did" in Egypt, but again a succession of words denoting audition follows: "Obey my *voice* and keep my *covenant* [the first covenant is the "ten *words*"] . . . These are the *words* which you shall *speak* . . . So Moses . . . *called* . . . and set before them *all these words* which the LORD has *commanded* him. And all the people *answered* . . . and *said*, 'All that the LORD has *spoken* we will do.' And Moses *reported* the *words* . . . And the LORD *said* . . ." (vss. 5-9). Israel understood her own history and discovered its meaning, to be sure, in the mighty acts of God—the Lord's acts as determined by the interaction of Word and word, and recognized as his acts only by the instrument of the Word.

Somewhere along the way there was a touch of the Deuteronomic literature, leaving the language of a few verses characteristically modified. The eloquent figure of the "eagles' wings" (vs. 4)

is movingly employed of the relationship of Israel to God in the
"Song of Moses" in Deuteronomy. The Lord found Israel

> . . . in a desert land,
>   and in the howling waste of the wilderness;
> he encircled him, he cared for him,
>
> . . . .
> Like an eagle that stirs up its nest,
>   that flutters over its young,
> spreading out its wings, catching them,
>   bearing them on its pinions,
>   the LORD alone did lead him . . . (Deut. 32:10-12).

Verses 5 and 6 of Exodus 19 should also be compared with Deuteronomy 26:18 and especially with Deuteronomy 7:6 and 14:2.
The Deuteronomists stress with some pride the conviction of
faith that Israel is a people chosen of God: ". . . the LORD your
God has chosen you to be a people for his own possession, out of
all the peoples that are on the face of the earth" (Deut. 7:6). All
of the strata of tradition show an awareness that "chosenness" is
God's Word and that the Word means service—Israel is chosen
by God to serve his inescapably universal purposes. The "Yah-
wist" historians convey this understanding of the Word of chosenness in the call of Abraham in Genesis 12:3: "by you all the
families of the earth shall bless themselves." The somewhat later
"E" material lifts up its Joseph figure to symbolize the Lord's chosenness, and sees fulfillment in the statement that not only Joseph
and his brothers and his father's house and Egypt were saved by
the fact of Joseph's chosenness, but *all the earth* came . . . to
Joseph to buy grain, because the famine was severe over all the
earth" (Gen. 41:57). Prophecy gives its most emphatic interpretation of the Word's chosenness in one of the Servant Songs, all
of which essentially deal with the meaning of chosenness and the
function of the entity chosen by the Lord (Isa. 42:1-7; 49:1-6;
50:4-9; 52:13—53:12). In language which appears strikingly to
give ultimate theological interpretation to the Joseph story, we
read:

> "It is too light a thing that you should be
>   my servant
> to raise up the tribes of Jacob
> and to restore the preserved of Israel;

> I will give you as a light to the nations,
>> that my salvation may reach to the
>>> end of the earth" (Isa. 49:6).

The Deuteronomists—far less lyrically, to be sure—possess and preach the same Word. Their insistence that Israel is a holy people, set apart, dedicated, consecrated, to the service of God, "a kingdom of priests and a holy nation" (Exod. 19:6; compare again Deut. 7:6 and 14:2, "For you are a people holy to the LORD . . .") makes essentially the same affirmation.

The Word of "chosenness" is subsequently affirmed as this Old Testament body of material dealing with the faith and life of the people of Israel is shaped in such a way as to affirm totally the hope and expectation of Israel's fulfillment of that Word. Thus there is produced in final fixed form a Testament which, while in no sense suppressing the human word, nevertheless gives predominant place to the divine Word, justifying on the whole the prophetic theme:

> It shall come to pass in the latter days
>> that the mountain of the house of the
>>> LORD
> shall be established as the highest of the
>> mountains,
>
> . . . .
> and all the nations shall flow to it,
>> and many peoples shall come, and
>>> say:
> "Come, let us go up to the mountain of
>> the LORD,
>> to the house of the God of Jacob;
> that he may teach us his ways
>> and that we may walk in his paths"
>>> (Isa. 2:2-3; see also Micah 4:1-4).

On the other hand, it is to be affirmed with equal force that this Testament is a testament of Word *and word;* that men persist here as everywhere, then as always, in representing their own, human word as his Word, in substituting thoughts for Thoughts and ways for Ways (see Rom. 1:18-23). It is the pride not alone of little Israel but of little Everyman to interpret God's seeking Love and confronting Presence and covenanting Proposal as the sign, guarantee, and promise of superiority and special privilege. It was true of the people of the Old Covenant. The same ones who understood, believed, and preserved the Word also passed on (sometimes surely believing) the word. It has not been and is not different in the New Covenant where, from the time of the disciples' association with the Word made flesh to the moving present, Word and word are not merely confused; sometimes the human word is given the authority of the divine Word.

It is evident here that Israel was absolutely clear herself about the character of the Word which she heard at Sinai: "All that the LORD has spoken we will do." We are ready to enter into Covenant—on his terms who initiates the Covenant (vs. 8). God's Word now promises an "appearance" (implicitly as tangible divine commitment to the Covenant); but it is to be a manifestation also by audition—"that the people may hear . . ." (vs. 9).

The People's Preparation (19:9b-15)

This description of preparatory rites for a ceremony reflects ancient religious practices and beliefs surviving from the past centuries of Israel's existence. The Lord will make himself manifest before all the people (vs. 11). A visual manifestation is anticipated: he will come "in a thick cloud" (vs. 9) "in the sight" of all (vs. 11). It is thus the Presence or the Glory—not the Person—that is seen (see also Isa. 6 and Ezek. 1).

Three days of ceremonial purification are required, including the washing of garments and sexual abstinence: one must come into the Presence "clean." Even so, on pain of death no one, man or beast, may approach too closely to the Presence (vss. 12-13). Old notions of "taboo" may still survive here; but even so we may well prefer this sense of appropriate distance between God and man to the all too common representations of chumminess which are characteristic of popular religion in our own days. To be sure, Christ gives us access to the Presence, but *we* must not confuse the Presence and the Person; we must not reduce God to any manifestation of him we are able to comprehend!

The narrative is shaped in a tradition which especially reveres the name, memory, and person of Moses. While Israel stands in awe, looking from afar, seeing and hearing at a well-calculated distance, Moses ascends to the very summit and into the cloud itself! The greatest tribute to Moses is preserved in the statement that the Lord "used to speak to Moses face to face, as a man speaks to his friend" (Exod. 33:11, possibly from E; the point, however, is not subscribed to by all strata of tradition—compare 33:20, possibly from J). The critical, inviolable power of the Presence, so strongly underlined in the prescribed preparation of the people, is to Moses uncritical, fully approachable, and benign; and in this implicit estimate of Moses we are confident that tradition remembers well and accurately.

The Lord's Commitment (19:16-25)

In the narrative of Israel's experiences at Sinai we find, by and large, a remarkably coherent, instructive account of the faith of Israel as Israel looks at her own past and the meaning of her continuing life. But verses 21-25 are another matter. It is likely that the section properly ends at verse 20, with Moses ascending Sinai at the call of the Lord. Verse 21, however, represents him as commanded to go right back down again to keep the foolish people from breaking through to stare at the Lord—and so perish! In the next verse the priests are warned to consecrate themselves or suffer the dire consequences of the Lord's fierce wrath, although presumably they would have joined in the people's consecration. The sense of verse 23 is that God must be reminded by Moses that he has already taken care of the matter (19:12). And verse 24 is concerned only to say that Aaron is the co-star with Moses in the Sinai act and, in distinction from verse 22, that Moses and Aaron alone with *no priests* attending, enter the Presence; and furthermore that any others attempting to join this company of two will find themselves "broken out against" by the Lord himself.

Now two positive statements are in order. Despite the long centuries of tradition's fluid, unceasingly changing form, and despite the fact that it passed through many minds and lips and hands, it is remarkable that such miscellaneous accumulations occur so infrequently. Second, such inconsequential confusion occasionally encountered reminds us that this whole treasure of the Word is given us in earthen vessels (II Cor. 4:7) and serves to check us sharply when and if we begin to equate the Word with the vessel which contains it. It is surely only the Living Word, the Third Party to our conversations with the Bible, who can help us in distinguishing the Word from the word, the communicated nature and will of God from the vessel which preserves it.

But there is emphatically none of this uncertainty in verses 16-20. Questions, yes. Are the natural phenomena to be interpreted as the violent manifestations of storm? Or erupting volcano? Or are these simply metaphors, intentional metaphors, to describe the otherwise indescribable—the sense of overpowering awe, mystery, and violently eruptive force in the actual Presence, in confrontation with the Glory of the Lord? There is a further persistent and often frustrating question: What is the relationship of the account to the actual episode?

Again, we must acknowledge that such questions as these cannot be answered conclusively. Granted that from the point of view of understanding the *faith* of ancient Israel these are not critical questions, we of typically Western frame of mind, who put so much significance upon delineation of fact, cannot but regret this kind of frustration. If it were conclusively demonstrable that tradition here preserves the eyewitness report of the sacred mountain under such violent natural seizure; and furthermore if such natural phenomena were unmistakably attributable to volcanic action (the strongest but still indecisive indication of this is the phrase in verse 18 "the smoke of it went up like the smoke of a kiln"), we could with some assurance locate Sinai-Horeb in the only area within possible range where volcanic phenomena have existed—that is, in the territory of ancient Midian (present Arabia) east of the northern end of the Gulf of Aqabah. Or if it could be shown conclusively that volcanic activity is *not* the explanation, but that what is literally described here is what is also literally and accurately recorded in the very old Song of Deborah (Judges 5), we should have strong, if not compelling, reason to locate Sinai in the general vicinity of Kadesh-Edom—somewhere to the south of the Dead Sea and north of the Gulf of Aqabah.

> "Lord, when thou didst go forth from
>   Seir,
>   when thou didst march from the region
>   of Edom,
> the earth trembled,
>   and the heavens dropped,
>   yea, the clouds dropped water.

> The mountains quaked before the LORD,
>   yon Sinai before the LORD, the God of
>   Israel" (Judges 5:4-5).

Or, if we *knew* that the description in Exodus 19 has no external (archaeological) relationship to place, time, and event and that it is simply and intentionally metaphorical, we would be afforded the luxury of shedding at least for the moment the responsibilities of geographer-topographer-historian; we could then read the passage in the knowledge that here at least no clues exist to aid in the possible reconstruction of an actual event.

But although these uncertainties of external structure remain, the account leaves uncomplicated and emphatic this "event" as internally apprehended—that is, as in faith remembered and appropriated and celebrated in that community which knew itself in subsequent centuries to be, as it were, the child of Sinai-Horeb. It is the faith of the community which came ultimately to read the meaning of its own life predominantly from that event. What is said in this record is said in faith. It is said categorically; it is put beyond the limits of dispute. It is affirmed colorfully, vividly, in descriptive language appealing to and involving *all* the senses: to every instrument of human perception God made known his Glory and Presence. It is still not himself that is perceived, but the unqualified fact of his now immediately impinging Life and Nature and Will.

What happened at Sinai constitutes an "appearance"—a "theophany." The appearance is emphatically not an end in itself, although the concluding verses (21-24) try very hard to make it so, but with notable lack of success. No. What is impressed on all is the awe and the magnitude and the certainty of the Presence at Sinai; but the basic motif of the account is the validation of the Word which is given there and of the Covenant which there comes into being.

Tradition deals here with Word and Covenant. It deals with what is to become in Israel's history the most important quality of its life— the Covenant quality. Israel is in time persuaded that what meaning her life bears is exclusively Covenant-meaning; and the Covenant between God and Israel is formally and tangibly brought into existence at Sinai. As remembered in the subsequent life of Israelism-Judaism, it is so overwhelmingly and powerfully *the* Covenant event that it tends to draw to itself, like a giant magnet, subsequent occasions and actions by which Covenant is further defined, redefined, expanded, and modified. This being the case, then, tradition must be concerned with more than validating the Word which is *Torah* (the divine instruction defining *Israel's* commitment and responsibility to Covenant); it is necessary also to affirm past any possible rebuttal that the Lord himself assumed the power and nature of his own commitment implicit in the revelation of his glory on Sinai-Horeb.

It is faith that is on record here. The Covenant is the subject. The Lord is Lord of nature, outside and above nature, more powerful than nature at its most powerful, able even to use nature's power as a cloak or a garment. This Lord, chiefly by the instrument of his Word, has created a people. Now by the same instrument, he initiates a Covenant, a God-People contract which is precisely defined in these simple terms: I will be *God* (a term without meaning except in relationship), bringing to this relational responsibility the qualities you experienced in the Egyptian deliverance and have overwhelmingly sensed in the revelation at Sinai; you will be *People* (a term also without meaning, biblically, except in relationship), bringing to this relational responsibility the performance of the Word (*Torah*) which is given here.

The Decalogue (20:1-17)

In a form differing only in a few details, this same series of statements appears again in Deuteronomy 5:6-21. What we call the "Decalogue" or the "Ten Commandments" is simply designated in the Old Testament as the "Ten Words" (34:28; Deut. 4:13; 10:4; see the marginal notes on these three verses). Such a compact definition of responsibility is by no means unique in the Old Testament. In Deuteronomy we find a series of vigorous prohibitions known as the "Twelve Curses" or "Dodecalogue"; they are "Twelve Words" delivered at Shechem, which was between Mount Ebal and Mount Gerizim (Deut. 27:12-26). It seems probable that in Exodus 21:12, 15-17 we have four surviving "words" from an originally longer series of offenses punishable by death. Leviticus 19:13-18 presents a series of ten or twelve items (depending upon how one divides the text) defining, largely by prohibition, the nature of social responsibility and concluding with the powerful statement later to be identified as "The Second Great Commandment" (Matt. 22:36-40; Mark

12:28-31). In ethical sensitivity and nobility it is a series unsurpassed in the Old Testament even by the Decalogue of Exodus 20 and Deuteronomy 5.

That the present form of the text means to present a list of *ten* commandments is certain. But on the precise counting of the ten, three different opinions have long been held. Briefly defined, and placed side by side, this is how the three suggested schemes appear:

	Judaism	Most of Protestantism. From Philo and Josephus to the ancient Church; Greek Orthodox; Reformed traditions	Augustine; Roman Catholic; and Lutheran	
I	vs. 1. I am the LORD	vs. 3. No other gods	vss. 3-6. No other gods and no images	I
II	vss. 3-6. No other gods and no images	vss. 4-6. No images	vs. 7. Name of the LORD	II
III		vs. 7. Name of the LORD	vs. 8. Sabbath	III
IV		vs. 8. Sabbath	vs. 12. Parents	IV
V		vs. 12. Parents	vs. 13. Murder	V
VI		vs. 13. Murder	vs. 14. Adultery	VI
VII		vs. 14. Adultery	vs. 15. Stealing	VII
VIII		vs. 15. Stealing	vs. 16. False Witness	VIII
IX		vs. 16. False Witness	vs. 17a. Covetousness (1)	IX
X		vs. 17. Covetousness	vs. 17b. Covetousness (2)	X

Any one of these arrangements of the Decalogue is obviously possible, and each has commended itself to large numbers of people. Judaism's conventional counting of the commandments will be followed in this discussion. It seems arbitrary to make a division in verse 17. The present form of the verse certainly represents an expansion of the original prohibition which, on the analogy of the four preceding prohibitions, probably read simply, "You shall not covet," or perhaps, "You shall not covet your neighbor's house" (that is, the totality of what is your neighbor's). Similarly, the separation of verse 3 from verses 4-6, and the making of two commandments out of the apparently single prohibition of other gods (vs. 3) and images (vss. 4-6), appear unjustified. Judaism's reckoning has been criticized on the ground that verse 1 is a declaration, not a commandment or prohibition; but it is certainly integral, the first necessary foundation "word" in support of the following, sequential nine "words."

Is the Decalogue Mosaic—did it originate in Moses' time? Not in its present form, according to many interpreters. This is not to deny the overwhelming testimony of tradition that Moses was a lawgiver, the author or mediator of *torah* (instruction). In ascribing the first five books of the Old Testament to Moses, ancient tradition attributes to him the accumulation and refinement of some eight centuries of *torah*—a fact which testifies to the strength of the memory of Moses' capacity as lawgiver. And in support of this, one may point to the obvious necessity of a constitutional body of instruction and control, a concrete, if initially simple, code of incorporation for the people.

But if we see no reason to doubt Moses' role in this regard, we must at once also concede the extreme difficulty of determining what—out of the extensive collection of *torah* attributed to him —is actually Mosaic. It may be pointed out that formal regulations obviously do not and cannot precede the conditions which it is their purpose to regulate. Thus, for example, traffic regulations do not precede the traffic problems with which they are concerned—unfortunately! In the same way, *torah* which is unquestionably aimed at conditions of monarchic political existence in Canaan (for example, instructions as to the appropriate conduct of the king himself in Deuteronomy 17:18-20), or at the control of problems demonstrably presupposing settled agricultural life (for example, the oft-repeated limitation on the gleaning of fields and vineyards, as in Deuteronomy 24:19-22 and Leviticus 19:9-10)—such *torah* can hardly be Mosiac in the literal sense.

Similarly, we may suppose that, *as presently formulated*, the commandments respecting Sabbath and parents and the prohibitions with regard to the making of images and to coveting are not Mosaic. Is it possible, then, that Moses was responsible for an original "ten words" on the order of verses 13, 14, and 15, each of which is in Hebrew two short words? The prudent answer to this question is that while this is possible, it does not appear probable. A more likely view, and one held by many competent interpreters, is that this present collection of ten commandments, this Decalogue, this aggregate of "ten words," probably represents not an original nucleus around which the growing fullness of Old Testament *torah* formed, not a chronologically prior basic code which was subsequently expanded, but rather a self-conscious, consummately discerning effort to reduce to its most significant essence a relatively comprehensive and detailed body of *torah*. In short, the Decalogue has been most competently interpreted as the summation of the will of the Lord for the community of Israel, drawn from an established body of legal and instructional material.

Now if this is true, it in fact enhances the importance of the Decalogue, for what is given is the deeply pondered, concentrated meaning of life under Covenant, as that meaning is apprehended in faith. To the possible objection that to regard the Commandments as a summation appears to reduce the Decalogue to merely human and therefore uninspired origin we should respond in vigorous denial: rather, this is to interpret the Word as we think the Word always comes—in interaction with the word. The Decalogue, so interpreted, *is* the Word; but more, it conveys the community's receipt of the Word and the community's response to the Word. The Lord has spoken: this is what we understand him to say; this is the significant minimum and essence which may not be further reduced; and this embraces his will for us.

If this interpretation is true, we can only say further that in a profound sense the Decalogue *is* Mosaic; what is formulated here in essence was certainly implicit in the words in and around which Moses first sought to order Israel's previously unordered existence. For the relationship of Israel to the Lord in a Covenant, the content of the Commandments was inherent from the beginning; the violation of any one of the "ten words" was from the beginning the violation of that relationship and that Covenant.

The Integrity of the Lord: The First Pentalogue (20:1-12)

The first five "words" have to do with that which is directly related to the Senior Party of the Covenant: God's (1) Identity, (2) Nature, (3) Name, (4) Day, and (5) Claim.

(1) The intensely concentrated definition of Covenant must first deal with the identity of the Initiator of the Covenant:

> "I am the LORD your God, who brought you out of the land of Egypt, out of the house of bondage" (20:2).

This definition of the Person of the Lord, this identification made in terms of Israel's own historical experience—this is itself a commandment. It demands: Know me and acknowledge me as the One without whom chaos would still embrace you, formless and void. Know me, for only in my Identity do you become an entity, only in my Identity can you be identified! Know me as Creator; but know me too as Deliverer, who brought you out of the "house of bondage," out of the condition of slavery. It was I who brought you from the closed to the open, from the bitter to the sweet, from the shackled to the free, from the lost to the saved! I am the Lord *your* God, who wrought this for *you!* Know me. Acknowledge me. Remember me. Know my *Identity*.

(2) The second Word continues: It is my *Nature* to be God alone. In the notion that there are other gods—although not in itself a denial of me—I am in fact denied, since this notion denies my Nature, and in this notion therefore I cannot *Be*.

> "You shall have no other gods before me. You shall not make for yourself a graven image, or any likeness of anything . . . you shall not bow down to them or serve them; for I the LORD your God am a jealous God, visiting the iniquity of the fathers upon the children . . . but showing steadfast love [devotion quite beyond the obligation of the relationship as such] to thousands of those who love me and keep my commandments" (20:3-6).

Elsewhere the same concept is affirmed in Israel's larger *torah* in a single remarkable sentence capable of sustaining four differing translations, which are nevertheless unified in meaning:

> The LORD our God is one LORD.
> The LORD our God, the LORD is one.
> The LORD is our God, the LORD is one.
> The LORD is our God, the LORD alone (Deut. 6:4; see margin).

It is the Lord's nature to be One, and Alone. And this nature of oneness-aloneness is such that it cannot in its very nature be represented; and since it cannot in its very nature be represented, *any* representation of it, in *any* form, is necessarily deceiving, untrue, and therefore prohibited. A vigorous (and ultimately fruitless) debate has been in process for years as to whether the prohibition of images could have become a part of Israel's traditional *torah* earlier than the time of the prophets of the eighth century B.C. There have always been some who have argued (inconclusively, we think) that in earlier times the Lord was represented in various forms. But there is no clear evidence anywhere in the Old Testament of an actual image of God that was not contemporaneously condemned. What we know of Israelite religion in its earliest expressions is consistent with the prohibition of images; and it is not an unreasonable inference that there would have been resistance to any representation of deity among the Israelites moving into Canaan—if only in defensive reaction to the vast variety of images in the many cults of the Canaanites.

Brief attention should be called to the characterization of the Lord as a jealous God. Perhaps this is in one sense a time-bound declaration; that is, perhaps something of Israel's unworthy exclusivism and pride is reflected here. On the other hand, if it is God's nature to be One-Alone-Unique, then it must also be his nature to be "jealous," which in this case means neither more nor less than to maintain this nature consistently. To condone an image—to be un-jealous—would be for God to deny himself. In later Judaism the interpretation of verse 5 held that the sins of the fathers are visited upon the children "when they retain the evil deeds of their fathers." And even when this is not the case, we must agree that there is a degree of bitter realism in the statement; children can and do suffer, sometimes generation upon generation, for the sins, the stupidities, the shortsightedness, and the selfishness of the fathers. Of course, we must acknowledge that men in all time have been far more ready to acknowledge God as Redeemer than as Judge, even though it should be obvious that if God is God he must be both! The expansion of the original commandment respecting the nature of God concludes on the note of his devotion to those who honor his nature.

(3) God's Identity; God's Nature; now God's Name:

"You shall not take the name of the LORD your God in vain;

for the LORD will not hold him guiltless who takes his name in vain" (20:7).

The "name" may not be treated lightly because it is inseparable from the reality. The name concerns the essence, the very being, of that which it identifies. To speak the name is to involve the person. More than this, when we push the matter of the name back to its most primitive conception, we find that "to name the name" is to seek to appropriate and command the power of the one named.

The most distant significance of this commandment lies shrouded in mystery. But we know that Israel occasionally did use (in transformed but still identifiable fashion) elements borrowed from the world of popular beliefs. The mark of this now dim world is still on the commandment concerning the name: men have sought to use the divine name, and even the name of "the LORD," to bring under their own control the power of the Deity, and so to coerce the unseen agent by knowing, speaking, and controlling the name. The *mark* of such superstitious magic, we may say, is still here; but the arrogant *intent* of magic is prohibited by the very commandment. The power of magic is denied. The would-be magician is implicitly threatened with death—as in 22:18 the death sentence is imposed on any sorceress.

And there is more than this. The commandment is the third "Word," coming after those referring to Identity and Nature. The "name" is the name of the Lord-Who-Created-You, of the Lord-One-Alone-Unique. It is this name which may not be taken in vain, which may not be uttered in trivial use, in prideful use, in use for personal gain and personal prestige or for the imposition of one's own will. And since, indeed, to know a name is to know identity and nature, no man *can* be guiltless who denies the Name by perverted use!

(4) To the first three "words" of Identity, Nature, and Name, a fourth is added concerning the Day that is the Lord's, or, better, the Day that is peculiarly his—for all are his.

"Remember the sabbath day, to keep it holy. Six days you shall labor, and do all your work; but the seventh day is a sabbath [the Hebrew word is directly related to the word for "seven"] to the LORD your God; in it you shall not do any work, you, or your son, or your daughter, your manservant, or your maidservant, or your cattle, or the sojourner

who is within your gates; for in six days the LORD made
heaven and earth, the sea, and all that is in them, and
rested the seventh day; therefore the LORD blessed the sabbath day and hallowed it" (20:8-11).

The form of the commandment in Deuteronomy 5:12-15 differs only in minor details from the first part, but after the phrase
"within your gates" it reads:

"that your manservant and your maidservant may rest as
well as you. You shall remember that you were a servant
in the land of Egypt, and the LORD your God brought you
out thence with a mighty hand and an outstretched arm;
therefore the LORD your God commanded you to keep the
sabbath day."

The seventh day is to be kept holy, that is, it is to be set apart
from the other days although "remembered" through all days.
The tasks of the week, fretful labor's anxious preoccupation with
the maintenance of life—all this is to be suspended every seventh
day in overt acknowledgment of the Lord and implicitly as a
declaration of trust in the Lord.

It is interesting and instructive to note that the two forms of
the Sabbath commandment seemingly stress different bases of
trust, appearing to establish two different primary grounds for
observing the Lord's Day. In Exodus it is the Creation faith that
is affirmed in the observance of the day, and one sees a very
close relationship between the present form of the commandment
and the story of creation in Genesis 1:1—2:4a (see especially
2:2-3). While this suggests that the *present form* of both these
passages is relatively late, it is not at all to say that either the
Creation faith or the Sabbath commandment is also relatively
late. Indeed there is every reason to believe that both concepts
appeared early in the structure of ancient Israel's faith and practice. In this coupling of Sabbath and Creation, faith is affirmed
in God's indisputable power, inherent in the nature and prerogatives of the Creator—power in and over the resources of man
and nature.

In Deuteronomy the appeal to Sabbath observance rests not
upon a primeval "event" but upon a historical event. The seventh
day's rest, in respect of *all* who labor, commemorates the days
of Egyptian bondage and remains a binding commandment be-

cause the observance constitutes an acknowledgment of God's
lordship and power over *all* conditions of servitude, and a confession of faith that Israel is God's people. Yet it remains essentially the *same quality* of faith in both forms of the statement of
the fourth commandment, since in Deuteronomy "sabbath" is
also an affirmation of the Creation faith. The observance is a
confession of faith that Israel is God's people, that she exists
because he brought her into existence in the deliverance from
Egypt. The fundamental sanction of the Sabbath in both statements
of the commandment, therefore, is *creation*—in Deuteronomy
the creation of a people, in Exodus the creation of the world.

To remember the Sabbath day and to keep it holy is to remember God as Creator and Sustainer and to acknowledge that
life continues under his reign and providence. More particularly,
and at its best and deepest understanding, the Sabbath is the perpetual reminder of the Covenant, not only with Israel but, through
Israel, with all the families of the earth.

The Christian observance of Sunday is, of course, not a sev-
enth- but a first-day observance. It is in the nature of a new
commandment, based on a New Covenant; but both the new
commandment and the New Covenant are fully appropriated only
out of the old to which they are related and which, in Christian
faith, they fulfill. The fact is that the Christian first-day observance
also commemorates Creation in a double sense. The first first-
day event was the day of Christ's resurrection, the first Easter
day. This is the Christian's deliverance from Egypt, this is his
redemption from chaos, this is his birth into life that is abundant
life, life in the present with indestructible meaning. This is for
every Christian a faith which is confirmed historically, in his own
experience of Christ. But the first day also commemorates the
Christian faith in the same Covenant proffered to all men—the
assurance climactically affirmed in Christ that he who creates is
also concerned, that he who is concerned also loves, that he who
loves *so* loves as to give his Son, and that so giving, he offers
through Christ the supreme gift of the Creator which is life forgiven, cleansed, fulfilled, and eternal.

(5) The structure of the Decalogue appears to be thoughtfully
wrought out and conceived as a concentrated statement of the
expansive body of Israel's *torah*—that body of instructional matter which has to do with the regulating of Israel's life in the

Covenant community and which was recorded as carrying in itself the authority of Moses and God.

The order and progression of the "ten words" is in no sense, then, accidental. From God's Identity the sequence moves through his Identity, his Nature, his Name, and his Day, to his *Claim:*

> "Honor your father and your mother, that your days may be long in the land which the LORD your God gives you" (20:12).

In view of all that inheres in the first four "words" and in the light of what is there already affirmed both explicitly and by inference; in consideration of ancient Eastern modes of thought and the characteristic psychological identification one always made of his own life with the life of immediate and also more distant progenitors; in recognition of the meaning of Covenant, together with Israel's faith in God's creation and his continuing exercise of the powers and prerogatives of Creator and Sustainer —in acknowledgment of all this it is apparent that the *intention* of the fifth commandment is to establish and perpetuate not merely the parental but by and through the parental the *divine* claim upon every life in Israel. It is, in effect, God's saying: "Your life is my gift. I created you in the image of the divine; the essential breath of-life is transmitted through your parents. In these regards, but surely not alone these, my life impinges directly upon your life. The life your parents bear and give to you is my life. To dishonor them is to dishonor me!"

One suspects that in our own society, as was also the case in ancient Israel but apparently to a much lesser degree, honoring of parents is withheld because this profoundly theological basis of honor is ignored or denied. It is the sense of the fifth commandment in its present place and sequence—taken, that is, in context—that parents are to be honored not in terms of their achievement as persons and parents, certainly not for reasons of sentiment, not at all because the practice is expedient in society or because common sense or common duty demands it. None of this. They are to be honored in acknowledgment of God's claim upon every individual life, in acknowledgment that all life is his and therefore sacred; and that the holiness of life can best be affirmed by honoring and respecting those two persons through whose combined life the divine image and animating breath are given.

The concluding phrase—peculiarly Deuteronomic in character —that in such honor one's day in the God-given land may be prolonged, need not be interpreted as an appeal to cheaper motives of reward. The motive was more noble; it is intended to affirm the proposition that in acknowledgment of this relationship of God-to-parents-to-child, and in appropriate acceptance of life as holy gift, life is lived in praise of God and therefore is fulfilled life, gratified life, meaningful life, completed life. In this sense, we think the phrase may sum up God's Pentalogue. Acknowledge and observe God's Identity, Nature, Name, Day, and Claim and it cannot be otherwise than that, in the land which "God gives you," the life which he presents and the existence which is of his ordering—that is, your days—will be "long." Your life will be fulfilled, abundant, and redeemed.

The Integrity of Israel: The Second Pentalogue (20:13-17)

The first five "words" of the Decalogue speak to the relationship between God and man in the Old Testament, which is the relationship of Israel to the Lord. It is a compact, five-member definition of the being and character of God himself, as he comes into relationship with, and lays responsibility upon, the Israelite. In these five essential respects the life and lordship of God are directly acknowledged in the life and service of Israel.

The second pentalogue, a series of five categorical prohibitions, voices succinctly and powerfully that which is destructive of the man-man relationship. Violation of any one of these prohibitions is violation of community. To perform or enact or perpetrate (Jesus added, of course, even to contemplate; see Matthew 5:21-46) any of these, is to introduce what is inevitably destructive of the man-man relationship and of the peaceful, co-operative, and productive coexistence of persons living in community, in critical, interdependent mutuality.

But let no one suppose that the second pentalogue is "secular" or "civil" as against a preceding religious or theological pentalogue. Nowhere in the Old Testament, or in the Bible as a whole, is human life seriously regarded as definable simply in terms of human relationships—that is, as a man-man relationship on a single horizontal plane. In the biblical faith, the horizontal relationship of man to man is what it is because of the vertical relationship of men to God. We may speak of a man-man relationship in the Bible, but it is prevailingly a God-man-man relationship. What one man is to another, what one person must assume and carry out with respect to another, is in ultimate analysis determined by the fact that both stand in primary relationship to God.

If, then, we speak of the second pentalogue as defining the integrity of the community of Israel, we must understand and take for granted the fact that Israel's integrity is a Covenant-integrity. Any words which attempt to order, guarantee, or maintain her productive life in community are also "theological" words, giving further form to faith in the Lord of the Covenant and in the Creator of Israel and the world.

It is in the light and meaning of God's Identity, Nature, Name, Day, and Claim—simply because God is God—that in the community of Israel there must be mutual, universal, inviolable respect of (6) life, (7) person, (8) property, (9) reputation, and (10) status.

(6) "You shall not kill" (20:13). The three prohibitions against murder, adultery, and theft appear in the Bible in varying order. In Luke 18:20 and Romans 13:9, for example, it is adultery, murder, theft. Hosea 4:2 equates lack of knowledge of God with, among other sins, "killing, stealing, and committing adultery." Jeremiah 7:9 lists "steal, murder, commit adultery," in a similar indictment. Ancient Greek translations of the Hebrew texts, both in Exodus and in Deuteronomy, also present variant orders for the three prohibitions. This is perhaps inevitable in the case of three such brief and tightly related restrictions.

The prohibition against killing is a defense of the integrity of a man's *life*. The term which is used does not have the limitation of the word "murder," which in current legal usage denotes the premeditated act of killing. In Deuteronomy 4:42 the same word is used of one "who kills his neighbor unintentionally." Every man's life is God's life (see the comment on 20:12), and no one, therefore, may violate the life of another.

In one of ancient Israel's oldest stories (Gen. 4:2-16), the tragic nature and consequences of this kind of violence are portrayed in the strange, brilliant account of the brothers, Cain and Abel (surely representing the close relatedness of human community). It is a story enacted in history over and over again, to man's continued anguish. One man, or one group, or one nation, or one race assumes arrogant power over the life of another; and God, also violated, must act in judgment. Not only is community destroyed, but loneliness and alienation ensue *precisely for the party perpetrating the violence!* Israel's historians read their own history in the sure understanding that to violate the integrity of another's life (and hence viciously and actively to deny community) is to bring the violator himself under the judgment of anguished alienation. An example of this is to be seen in the virtual collapse of King David's hitherto phenomenally beneficent existence, for his total reign is interpreted as having turned on the Bathsheba incident, combining murder, coveting, theft (of a man's wife), adultery, and even in a sense false witness (see II Sam. 11). The same understanding of murder as disruptive of community and as violation of God is to be seen in the account of Naboth, Ahab, and Jezebel in I Kings 21.

The commandment denies the right of any man to take the life of another. Life is God's. Only he may give it. Only he may take it away. Converted to positive terms, this prohibition would maintain the integrity of the individual life as basic to the functioning of community, both man-man and God-man.

Jesus, in the New Testament, reiterates the prohibition against killing, and he sensitively extends it to its ultimate limit. This commandment can be violated not only overtly but as well *in mind* and in intention (Matt. 5:21-24).

(7) "You shall not commit adultery" (20:14). If life is to be held inviolable in the community, so is the *person*. The two stories of creation (Gen. 1:1—2:4a and 2:4b-25) lay strong emphasis on the differentiation and function of sex: as the life itself is creatively given of God, so also is the sex. That which is involved in the distinction of man and woman, male and female, is purposively and functionally given; and the abuse of that purpose and function involves violation of the Giver as well as of both persons involved. And since the prohibition specifically deals with adultery (implying the violation of marital relationships) rather than fornication (although this is surely also, by intention, prohibited in the commandment), the integrity of three and even four persons may be involved in a single case of adultery.

In the full Old Testament context adultery, the fundamental disrespect and violation of person, not only destroys the human community; like the violent act of the destruction of the life of another, it is also destructive of the God-man relationship. One cannot mistake in the David-Bathsheba story the historian's sense of broken communion between king and God (see especially II

Sam. 12:13) as well as of the wretchedly abused Covenant community (Bathsheba's husband, originally a Hittite, is a natural-
ized Israelite who has taken a name compounded with the divine
name—Uri-Yah, "The Lord is my light!"). The classic Old
Testament declaration is put on the lips of Joseph who, on
grounds of respect both for the husband and the woman, rejects
the invitation to adultery and also cries, ". . . how then can I
do this great wickedness, and sin against God?" (Gen. 39:9).

(8) "You shall not steal" (20:15). This prohibition is a defense of a man's *property*. It cannot be interpreted in such a way
as to support an economic system which facilitates the acquisition by a relatively few of a nation's or a people's wealth. It cannot
be taken to sanction the accumulation of goods and possessions
and economic power in disproportionate, and inevitably unjust
and unrighteous, measure by attempting to restrain, on divine
authority, those whose rights have been fundamentally abused in
the process. On the other hand, the creation and perpetuation of
the prohibition is certainly not due merely to an attempt of a
wealthy class in Israel to protect their property.

This commandment is linked with the two which precede it.
In the relative poverty which prevailed in the ancient East there
was, of course, a more direct identification of a person with his
property than is true today; and this was no doubt due in part to
the dependence of the person upon certain minimal possessions
for his very life—his subsistence and his continuation in existence.
For the overwhelming majority of people in all the world's history, life has been and still is quite without the "cushions" to
which we have become accustomed, that is, such things as sav-
ings, or the privilege of credit, to say nothing of socially created
buttresses against the fundamental threats of hunger and the
elements. In a time which did not know modern medicine, the
theft of a garment, put aside during a warmer day, could result
not only in the owner's bitter suffering from cold through the
night, but actually to complications leading even to death. Or
the theft of a meager flock, by which a shepherd eked out a
literal hand-to-mouth existence, could easily result in intense suffering from malnutrition for the shepherd and his family, always
undernourished at best, if not in the actual loss of one or more
members of the family.

In a society where property and life are thus immediately related, the prohibition against theft is certainly not primarily de-

signed to protect the accumulated wealth—whether well-gotten or ill-gotten—of society's small minority of economic barons. This prohibition is as serious and significant as the two preceding prohibitions in defense of life and person and is at one with them. In a society where virtually all property is in an immediate sense the means of subsistence rather than items of mere convenience or luxury or pleasure or whim, to steal is potentially as great a violation of human integrity as to murder or to commit adultery.

In the biblical faith, which in multiple ways affirms that "the earth is the LORD's and the fulness thereof" (Ps. 24:1) and which understands community finally in terms of the God-man-man relationship, to take what is another's—be it life, person, or property—is, of course, to take what is Another's: it is to violate God.

It is the interesting opinion of some interpreters that the original form of the prohibition against stealing is still preserved in Exodus 21:16 (as the third in a surviving fragment of four offenses punishable by death):

> "Whoever steals *a man*, whether he sells him or is found in possession of him, shall be put to death."

We have now no way of proving whether this was the original formulation of the prohibition or not, but we can easily understand the importance of such a prohibition in a very simple nomadic or semi-nomadic society, where the vast bulk of property was the communal possession of the tribe as a whole, and in an age when a slave was a common and valuable marketable item (as was still true in the United States as of about a hundred years ago). In such times man-stealing offered the greatest reward for the risk involved and constituted the grounds for Israel's first commandment against theft.

The matter is raised here not merely for reasons of academic interest, but to underline again the more profound and theological understanding of the act of stealing. It is possible that the more general prohibition in the succinct commandment "You shall not steal" *bears still* the weight of indictment in man-stealing; as interpreted here, stealing is as direct and as powerful an assault on human integrity and the God-man-man community as is murder or adultery.

(9) "You shall not bear false witness against your neighbor" (20:16). The neighbor's *reputation* must not be violated. If it is

true, as seems probable, that the Decalogue is an effort to compress an established, formalized, and extensive *torah*—that is, a body of instruction—what is given pointed summary in this prohibition?

Certainly the language of the ninth commandment suggests juridical practice. "To bear false witness" is to give false testimony in court (the word in the text is literally "to answer"). It is, therefore, unquestionably the sense of the prohibition that formal "witness" must for no reason be inaccurate. In this sense it can be argued that the commandment is only indirectly concerned with a man's reputation, and that its primary motivation is the defense of the integrity of the judicial system.

This is true enough; but at the same time it appears that the commandment intentionally embraces a broader and more general element of *torah*. The essential relationship in the Covenant community is God-man-man, or man-God-man, which is simply to say again that men stand in relationship to one another only as both stand in immediate relationship to God. Rights are never merely human rights. Faith in God as Creator and Sustainer implies that rights which pertain to man are divine rights in the sense that God bestowed them. Again, as in the case of life, person, and property, reputation may not be falsely violated without also violating God and the aggressor's own relationship with God. And there is no doubt whatsoever that the prohibition intends to suppress any and all "answers" that constitute false testimony against the neighbor.

Such non-specifically juridical words of the broader *torah* as these are implicit in the commandment:

> "You shall not utter a false report. You shall not join hands with a wicked man, to be a malicious witness. You shall not follow a multitude to do evil [all of this is in the nature of general admonition against damaging words: and now the same passage turns to formal legal consideration]; nor shall you bear witness in a suit, turning aside after a multitude, so as to pervert justice; nor shall you be partial to a poor man in his suit [if formal false witness may not damage the innocent it must also refrain from endorsing the guilty]" (Exod. 23:1-3).

The same juxtaposition of informal with formal incriminating words appears in one of the commandments and prohibitions listed in Leviticus 19:13-18:

> "You shall not go up and down as a slanderer among your people, and you shall not stand forth [this is juridical language] against the life of your neighbor: I am the LORD" (Lev. 19:16).

The sense of the ninth commandment as summation is clear: in no way whatsoever may one falsify his witness, his report, even his casual conversation, about another. To do so is to violate that which a man *is*, and it is therefore a violation not only of the two-member, man-man relationship, but of the three-member, God-man-man community.

> (10) "You shall not covet your neighbor's house; you shall not covet your neighbor's wife, or his manservant, or his maidservant, or his ox, or his ass, or anything that is your neighbor's" (20:17).

This final commandment, the fifth prohibition in the second pentalogue, has also almost certainly been expanded since its original formulation. But its intent is consistent with the four preceding "words" in defense of life, person, property, and reputation. As no one may assume arbitrary damaging rights over the essential qualities of another's being, so the full *status* of a man—all that is implicit in the word "house"—must be inviolable, not only from physical or material injury, from any kind of overt abuse, from any explicit, assessable damage, from another's appropriation, but (remarkable concept!) from another's *wish* to appropriate, another's *thought* of appropriation, another's envious dream of appropriation—in short, from another's covetousness.

Biblical *torah* repeatedly finds modern counterparts in the complex systems of Western law. But legal systems as such do not produce anything that corresponds to the biblical sensitivity which forcefully enjoins against the *source* of all violence, namely, the realm of thought and contemplation, the intangible but critically powerful world of human imagination.

Just as the fifth commandment of the first pentalogue bears a climactic and summary relationship to the four preceding commandments (see comment on 20:12), so this injunctive word against illicit traffic through the mind is sum and climax of the pentalogue in protection of Israel's integrity. As climax, it conveys the sure knowledge that the overt act in perversion of justice stems from the unseen recesses of mind and imagination, where in contemplation the perversion is already effected. As summary and condensation of the broad *torah*, it stands in direct or indirect relationship to many commandments which have nothing directly to say about covetousness as such. Many which ostensibly regulate overt conduct have unmistakable implications for what a man thinks in his heart. One recalls, for example, the law in Exodus 23:4-5 (see comment) respecting one's obligation when confronted with one's enemy's straying ox or overburdened ass. Whether one acts in such a situation justly, or by inaction perverts justice, is entirely determined by the way in which the neighbor's "house" is contemplated in the mind. If contemplation is covetous, community is already violated and all possibility of mutuality is crushed.

More directly, the prohibition of covetousness embraces and condenses the meaning of the most sensitive and penetrating item in all of Israel's *torah*, from that same list of "words" in Leviticus 19:

> "You shall not hate your brother in your heart, but you shall reason with your neighbor, lest you bear sin because of him. You shall not take vengeance or *bear any grudge against* the sons of your own people, but you shall love your neighbor as yourself: I am the LORD" (Lev. 19:17-18).

The Ten Commandments, then, comprise two pentalogues: one purposes to maintain the integrity of God, the Author of the Covenant with Israel; the other is concerned with the community thus created and with that community's integrity *thus defined*. This collection out of Israel's full *torah* is thought to convey the very essence of God's total will with respect to his own Person but also, and at the same time, with respect to every other Covenant person. The place of the Decalogue in the life of ancient Israel, then, can hardly be overemphasized. Once formulated, it was understood and celebrated in Israel as itself a major "event," almost on a par with and inseparably linked to the event of Israel's deliverance from Egypt. In the same way it is a "celebration" event, disclosing the fact, and the meaning and purposiveness, of Israel's election by the Lord.

It would appear that this "event" of the Decalogue came to be celebrated in Israel sometime after the origin of the very ancient confessions of Israel's faith which move from the event of the Exodus by God's mighty hand and outstretched arm directly to God's gift in the possession of Canaan. Examples of such early confessions are found in Deuteronomy 6:21-25 and 26:5-9 and, in considerably expanded form of the same essential confession, in Joshua 24:2-13 (see especially verses 7-8). The form of this essential credo is very early indeed and may have had its original formulation (in a much simpler version) as early as, or not long after, the firm establishment of monarchy in the tenth century B. C.

Finally, it must be insisted that this central Covenant event of God's disclosure of his will *is* in a real sense Mosaic. Moses returned with his liberated people to worship God at the same mountain where first his own little shell of finitude was invaded by the Word: "Moses, Moses!" And as Moses knew would be the case, Israel's communal enclosure was in terrifying certitude penetrated by the same Word—a Word *in fact* ultimately responsible for the "ten words," a Word in equal fact which was to appear in the fullness of God's time as the Word made flesh.

The Ordering of Covenant Life (20:18—23:33)

Introduction to Torah (20:18—21:1)

The first and oldest code of instruction in the Old Testament, known as the Covenant Code, is contained in chapters 20-23 of Exodus. The relatively brief section in 20:18—21:1 is apparently transitional, like a bridge: it serves as a conclusion to the scene of chapter 19 and as a religious addition to the Decalogue (it restates the prohibition against images and sets certain limitations with respect to the building of an altar); at the same time it serves as an introduction to the Covenant Code.

Verses 18-22 resume the narrative interrupted by the Decalogue. We stand again with ancient Israel before the sacred mountain, Sinai-Horeb, which is now in violent seizure (thunder, lightning, trumpet sound, smoke). This is God on the mountain. It is the appearance of God. Or it is that which accompanies his Presence, the actualization of his Voice, his Word. For ordinary men it is an occasion of fear. The role and stature of Moses are again emphasized. "You speak to us," the people cry, "... but let not God speak to us, lest we die" (vs. 19). And Moses, with a word of reassurance for his people, ascends the mountain, disappears in the cloud, and receives the Word.

The transition adds to the categorical and broadly inclusive prohibition of images (20:3-6) the seemingly unnecessary itemization of "gods of silver" and "gods of gold." But in verses 24-26 there is incorporated a very ancient prescription concerning altars, which reflects simple tastes and which stands through all the years of ancient Israel's life as a vigorous reminder of her earliest days as a Covenant People.

The altar is the focal point of communion of God and man, and of man and man together with God. An altar may be absolutely anywhere, since it may be made of earth. Wherever the altar is, the Lord's name is there "remembered," and the Lord bestows his blessing. In this very old prescription only two simple sacrifices are called for: the burnt offering (the complete consumption by fire of an animal victim), signifying the worshiper's homage to the god-ness of God; and the peace offering, a joyous, religious, communion meal celebrating the full three-member relationship of the Covenant by enacting the oneness at the common board of the Lord with his people, and his people with each other.

If an altar is to be built and worship is to be entered upon in any area where stones are at hand, these may be employed in the making of the altar. But the same rule of uncompromised simplicity still holds: the stones may not be hewn; they may not be fashioned or worked or tooled. And the altar itself must be unassuming, unimposing, and modest, accessible without steps which would expose the "nakedness" of those directly serving at the altar (see 28:40-43, where short skirts are later forbidden for the officiating priests).

This is an early and effective way of saying that what is important in worship of God is the fact and content of the worship itself. It forms an early and discerning protest against the powerful and perennial tendency in every cult, ancient or modern, so to proliferate, so to elaborate, so to glorify the total "equipment" of worship as to make of worship's material representation an end in itself. These prohibitions of immodesty and pretension in and at the altar were not uncommonly violated in ancient Israel. The careful insistence upon properly modest dress for the priests (28:40-43) bears the mark of some adjustment: the fault in the elevated altar, so it came to be reasoned, was merely in the priests' embarrassment, a matter to be remedied not by a more modest altar but by the priests' more discreet apparel. Exodus 27:1-8 and Ezekiel 43:13-17 are more open testimony to an irrepressible disposition to elaborate the structure of the altar. On the other hand, Joshua 8:30-31 and I Kings 18: 31-32 both recall in different epochs the ancient demand for the unpretentious altar.

On Servitude and Freedom (21:2-11)

While it is not always possible to define the extent of Israel's "borrowing," she *did* draw from the common practice (as defined both by custom and law) of the people already resident in Canaan upon her entrance. And indirectly, through them, she drew from the common custom and law dominant in the ancient Near and Middle East of that day. It is necessary, however, to add the unqualified judgment that what Israel borrowed she always transformed in significant degree; which is to say that what Israel took over she modified by incorporating it into the total structure of faith and the Covenant community.

Israel met the crises of her existence—which was suddenly made unfamiliar and vastly more complex when the people settled in Canaan—by adopting many formal regulations already and for long successfully in operation there. From 21:2 to 22:16 the Covenant Code presents laws which must have been predominantly "borrowed" from Canaanite practice, and borrowed very early for the most part—that is, in the two centuries immediately following Israel's entrance into Canaan and before the establishment of the monarchy under Saul, David, and Solomon in the eleventh and tenth centuries.

From 22:17 to 23:19 religious regulations are dominant. These, apparently, more directly express the original character and mind of Israel. The concluding section of the Covenant Code, 23:20-33, is cast in the form of divine speech, assuring Israel of the nature and reality of the Covenant:

> "You shall serve the LORD your God, and I will bless your bread and your water ... I will fulfil the number of your days" (23:25-26).

In *present* form the Covenant Code is no older than this latest concluding section, but this can hardly be later (at the very latest) than the middle of the eighth century. But the Code as a whole embraces a span of many centuries, reaching back into both preoccupation Canaan and pre-Mosaic religion. Its formulation and preservation, all in all, represent a stupendous achievement.

It is altogether appropriate that the Code opens on the theme of servitude and freedom: it follows immediately upon the record of the experiences of Israel in both states of existence. The section, verses 2-11, is in two parts, dealing respectively with the male and the female slave.

Verses 2-6, dealing with the male slave, provide freedom in the seventh year for a Hebrew slave, who leaves as he came, whether single or married. If he has been married during slavery, he may leave alone; or, electing to remain, he commits himself in an appropriate ceremony to lifetime slavery (vs. 6). The same law in the Code of Deuteronomy (15:12-18) reflects a marked refinement of feeling which must have taken place in the intervening years (possibly during late eighth and early seventh centuries). There continued slavery remains an option, but, at least inferentially, the slave is freed with all his family. And what is more,

> ". . . when you let him go free from you, you shall not let him go empty-handed; you shall furnish him liberally out of your flock, out of your threshing floor, and out of your wine press; as the LORD your God has blessed you, you shall give to him" (Deut. 15:13-14).

And why? What is the ground and justification for such liberality with the slave?

> ". . . if your brother becomes poor beside you, and sells himself to you, you shall not make him serve as a slave: he shall be with you as a hired servant and as a sojourner. . . . For they are my servants, whom I brought forth out of the land of Egypt; they shall not be sold as slaves" (Lev. 25:39-42; see also Deut. 15:15).

Female slavery in Exodus 21:7-11 is not what it is for the male. The term for slave here is "concubine," and this is the relationship contemplated between the master and the female slave. There is no parallel to this regulation in other codes of the Old Testament, and the rights here maintained for the woman are remarkable. "If she does not please her master" she may not be sold as a slave, but may only be "redeemed," presumably by her family or by another who will bring her into the same relationship. And,

strikingly, her master under these circumstances is deemed to
have "dealt faithlessly with her." If the female "slave" is given to
the master's son, she becomes as the master's daughter! If the
master-husband takes "another wife" (the "slave" is inferentially
a wife), the concubine may leave without penalty if she is in the
least neglected as to food, clothing, or marital relationship.

Israel's life must be seen and comprehended against the broader
background of the ancient Near and Middle East; when so viewed
it is indisputable that the religion of Israel refined and even transformed much that she inevitably took over from her total environment. It is the sense of Covenant, of God's presence and holiness, of the relationship between God and people, and of God's
grace and redemption experienced in history, which is responsible
for the remarkable disposition and rights of slaves in the Old
Testament (see also Exod. 12:43-44; 21:20-21, 26-27; Deut. 12:
17-18; 16:10-11; 23:15-16; Lev. 25:10).

On Control of Violence (21:12-36)

What is apparently the mutilated torso of an originally longer
code still survives in 21:12 and 15-17 in four "words" which im-
pose the death penalty for murder (see also Gen. 9:6; Lev. 24:17;
Num. 35:30-31), for physical violence against parents, for man-
stealing, and for verbal abuse (cursing) of parents. These four
brief, unqualified declarations ("whoever ... shall be put to
death") must have been a part of a decalogue or of a dodecalogue
(12 laws). The first of these four has been expanded (vss. 13-14)
to distinguish between voluntary and involuntary manslaughter.
If death is accidentally inflicted (expressed in the phrase "God
let him fall into his hand") the inadvertent killer may take refuge
—in early times at any altar of the Lord anywhere, and later,
when the one Jerusalem altar replaced all others, in any one of
several designated cities of refuge (Deut. 4:41-43; 19:1-3; Num.
35:9-15; and Joshua 20:1-9). Here, for example, is the word of
the Lord to Joshua:

> ". . . 'Appoint the cities of refuge . . . that the manslayer who
> kills any person without intent or unwittingly may flee there;
> they shall be for you a refuge from the avenger of blood' "
> (Joshua 20:2-3).

The old, primitive principle of blood revenge (see the vicious and
very ancient Song of Lamech in Genesis 4:23-24) has always clung

tenaciously, even to relatively sophisticated societies down to our own day. Obviously it persisted also in Israel.

Israel's powerful feelings about the sacredness and significance of the parental relationship are of course made explicit in one of the "words" of the Decalogue (see the comment on 20:12). Here to strike or curse either parent is a capital offense (vss. 15, 17; on the whole question of the appropriate honoring of parents see also Deut. 5:16; 21:18, 21; 27:16; Lev. 19:3a; 20:9).

Manstealing, that is, any form of kidnapping, is also punishable by death. The original form of the declaration in 21:16 appears to have been expanded by the addition of the explanation, "whether he sells him or is found in possession of him." In the opinion of some this may be the original sense of the prohibition against stealing in 20:15, a judgment which in any case underlines the great antiquity of the sentence. Deuteronomy 24:7 preserves a later reformulation:

> "If a man is found stealing one of his brethren, the people of Israel, and if he treats him as a slave or sells him, then that thief shall die; so you shall purge the evil from the midst of you."

In common with ancient Hittite and Babylonian laws, the Covenant Code provides compensation for injury inflicted, and for time lost in recuperation and convalescence (vss. 18-19). Punishment, here unstipulated, must be inflicted for the death of a slave from a beating (vss. 20-21); and yet, oddly enough, if the slave survives the beating for even a day or two, punishment of the owner's brutality is waived on the ground that he has lost his property, which apparently is regarded as penalty enough! Here, of course, the law is in conflict with itself over two opposing principles: a slave is at once human life and mere property. If we look at verses 26-27, which may well have been at one time connected with verses 20-21, we will understand that in Israel the first principle became and remained dominant: if the slave's owner should inflict the loss of an eye or even a tooth upon the slave, the slave must be given his freedom in compensation!

In verses 22-25 the famous *lex talionis*, the law of retaliation, is given setting and declaration (see also Lev. 24:18-21 and Deut. 19:15-21). The actual statement of the proposition, "eye for eye, tooth for tooth," appears in a particular case setting: a pregnant woman is injured by men in strife. Miscarriage results but no other harm. The person responsible pays a fine proposed by the husband and subject to the approval of judges. "If any harm follows" (in addition to miscarriage), it must be then "life for life, eye for eye," and the like.

Two observations are in order. Looked at from the perspective of concepts of justice prevailing *before* the formulation of the *lex talionis*, this is properly seen as a significant advance, firmly and humanely limiting the imposition of damages: under this restriction the vindictive man of power is prevented from extorting exorbitant damages—for example, from taking the life of one who inflicts upon him or upon a member of his family only relatively minor injury. The law thus appears in the ancient world in wide application a thousand years before the time even of David and Solomon.

It is also emphatically to be observed that in very fact the principle of exact retaliation is *not* normative in the Old Testament; that the law is demonstrably of Canaanite formulation as it appears here, borrowed for an interim period by Israel, and retained only for certain particular cases as a norm of judgment in specific instances of injury. We think it is no accident that it appears in this setting; apparently this is one of those few cases in which the law remained applicable.

The same thing is to be said of the other two contexts in which the law of retaliation appears in the Old Testament. In Leviticus 24:18-21, in the case of a beast, it is life for life. This is, strictly speaking, beside the point. But in verses 19-20 the principle of exact retaliation is applied to physical, bodily disfigurement, and the sense is of deliberate disfigurement premeditatedly and maliciously inflicted. Under these circumstances, then,

> ". . . as he has done it shall be done to him, fracture for fracture, eye for eye, tooth for tooth; as he has disfigured a man, he shall be disfigured."

Deuteronomy 19:15-21 makes the point even more emphatic that *lex talionis* is in Israel not a universally binding principle, but an ancient item of elemental justice still appropriate and applicable only in certain particular judgments. Here the despicable witness maliciously perverts his testimony so as to bring injury upon his innocent "brother." Under these circumstances, in this particular case,

"... if the witness is a false witness and has accused his brother falsely, then you shall do to him as he had meant to do to his brother; so you shall purge the evil from the midst of you. And the rest shall hear, and fear, and shall never again commit any such evil among you. Your eye shall not pity; it shall be life for life, eye for eye, tooth for tooth, hand for hand, foot for foot."

Israel's law and all her *torah* is Covenant law, Covenant *torah*. In Covenant life, in Covenant meaning, in Covenant regulation, the primary *quality* is set by God himself. In Covenant law—as is also the case in Covenant history—the mercy and gentleness and forgiveness and redemption of God are known, repeatedly and marvelously tempering the rigidity of the older principle of exact retaliation. (But see also what Jesus does with this in Matthew 5:38-42!) But the purity and the righteousness of God are also known and seriously regarded as imposing demands upon the Covenant community. And where his purity and righteousness are most brutally and maliciously repudiated, then—against the surging indignation which would exact exorbitant payment of damages—let it be *only* in the exact measure, specifically, "eye for eye ..."

Verses 28-36 continue the general theme of penalties for physical violence, but the focus shifts to the ox. Verses 28-32 prescribe procedures of justice applicable in the case of the goring ox, whose owner is thus fixed with dire responsibility (vs. 29). Incidentally, in this section the slave is regarded merely as property (vs. 32).

The ox remains the subject in verses 33-36, but in verses 33-34 the animal is the victim, not the culprit. In verses 35-36 it is ox against ox and owner against owner.

The ox remains the subject in 22:1; but it is well to follow the chapter division because the theme of physical violence, dominant down to chapter 22, here gives way in the main to regulations of a broader and less personal character.

On General Conduct and Responsibility (22:1—23:33)

These two chapters fall into three sections. The first, 22:1-17, differs from the second, 22:18—23:19, both in form and content. The first section is characterized by the formula, "If so-and-so ... he (the offender) shall do thus-and-so ..." This is termed "casuistic" law, and is generally thought to have been derived largely from the Canaanites; for the most part it has to do with what we should commonly call secular rather than specifically cultic or religious matters. The second section employs the "if" form occasionally (as in 22:25; 23:4), but with the second person "you" instead of the third person "he." It is characterized throughout by what is called the "apodictic" law—that is, the non-casuistic, non-theoretical formulation, the flat, unqualified, direct commandment or prohibition. Apodictic law has to do with specifically cultic or theological matters (for example, 22: 20); it is implicitly much more closely related to the religion of the Covenant community. It is, as such, much more characteristically Israelite in origin and character.

The third section in this block of material, 23:20-33, is in the form of a hortatory speech of the Lord. In its present form it is later than the preceding laws of the Covenant Code and was affixed to this code sometime after its present organization. A detailed comparison of the three sections follows.

Exodus 22:1-17. The Revised Standard Version has restored to a more logical order the first four verses by placing verses 2-3a (which interrupt the subject of appropriate restitution for stolen animals and justify the slaying of a thief for robbery by night but not by day) after verse 4.

Matters of proper restitution then continue to be the subject throughout this section:

for crop damage by loose, foraging animals—restitution by the owner of the animal or animals (vs. 5);

for the loss of grain by fire—restitution by the one setting the fire (vs. 6);

for theft of property committed to a neighbor's trust—restitution by the thief (double) if apprehended; or if not, inferentially but in unspecified fashion, by the neighbor if, when he comes "near to God," it is shown that he is himself guilty (guilt or innocence apparently to be determined at the sanctuary either by oracle [sacred lots?] or by oath) (vss. 7-8);

for any disputed breach of trust—restitution (double) by the one of the two parties pronounced guilty "before God" (vs. 9);

for the loss of an animal committed to a neighbor's trust— no restitution by the neighbor if through an "oath by the LORD" (before God) the trustee is shown to be innocent or the loss is demonstrably accidental; but if guilty and/or responsible, the neighbor-trustee must make restitution (vss. 10-13);

for damage to or destruction of anything borrowed—full restitution by the borrower, unless the owner was with it, or it (the damaged or destroyed property) was rented, in either of which cases it is the owner's loss (vss. 14-15);

for forcing a virgin—restitution by the aggressor male, the act of marriage or, if unacceptable, "money equivalent to the marriage present for virgins" (vss. 16-17).

These are casuistic laws. They are laws clearly under lay auspices and jurisdiction. There is nothing peculiarly Israelite about them; indeed, parallels to laws such as these appear in profusion over the ancient East and in considerably expanded form, for example, in the Code of Hammurabi of Babylon (eighteenth century, B.C.). In these laws the Lord plays no direct role. (The phrase "an oath by the LORD" in verse 11 is an Israelite addition, or modification.) If the deity is mentioned it is only by the general name for God ("Elohim," as in verses 8 and 9); any theological or ethical content is extremely weak. These are laws commonly current over the broad area into which Israel came; and she took them over in the years between conquest and monarchy.

Exodus 22:18—23:19. Even the most casual reader of the Covenant Code cannot fail to observe the change in the *form* of statement beginning in 22:18. In quick succession three offenses are brought under categorical sentence of death—sorcery, perverted sex act (with an animal), and idolatrous sacrifice. The gender of the first offender is feminine ("sorceress"). So it is in I Samuel 28 (where, very early, sorcery is outlawed, but in vain), and so also in Jeremiah 7:18 and 44:15. But sorcery is also known in the Old Testament as a male occupation (for example, see Lev. 20:27; Deut. 18:10; and Mal. 3:5).

Satisfaction of the sexual appetite by intercourse with beasts is regarded as a capital offense also in Leviticus 20:15-16 and Deuteronomy 27:21. This, like the prohibition of sorcery, has a strong theological relationship. All efforts in any way to probe or influence the unseen and the unknown—other than by the established functions of the prophet and the priest—are prohibited on the primary ground that such constitutes an illegitimate invasion of the exclusive domain of God. Divination, witchcraft, sorcery, necromancy—all these stand in defiance and violation of the God-man relationship, and are *therefore* anathema. This sensitive understanding of *faith* was doubtless given added support by restrictions rooted in expediency and motivated by the prevalence of the magical and the occult in surrounding religions which were always in some measure competitors. But while, for example, Hittite (not Babylonian) law also places this kind of debased sex act under sentence of death (vs. 19), in the context of Israelite apodictic law the prohibition must be understood as being rooted in the same essential theological perspective as the immediately preceding and following prohibitions against sorcery and idolatrous sacrifice. To be an Israelite is to be a Covenant person in relationship to the Lord; and thus to debase and pervert that human function by which the Covenant community continues to reproduce itself—and so to perpetuate within itself the life of God—is to deny the Covenant, the God-man relationship, and God himself.

The third prohibition (22:20) puts idolatrous sacrifice under sentence of death. It is the most vehement of the three. In some circles today it would be termed an intolerant prohibition. But this is a part of Israel's apodictic law, a part of that element in her legal, formal *torah* which is distinctively her own. The prohibition is laid down in the midst of a people whose confession of faith is that "the LORD . . . saw our affliction . . . and the LORD brought us out of Egypt . . . into this place" (Deut. 26:7-9). The people are his by right of redemption, as well as by creation and sustenance. Hence, "Whoever sacrifices to *any* god, save to the LORD only, shall be utterly destroyed" (vs. 20).

Verses 21-24 cite three classes of persons repeatedly given special mention in Old Testament law—the stranger (here it is the word more commonly rendered "sojourner"), the widow, and the orphan (or, often, "the fatherless"). These are all persons who must live without the crucial support given by the male head of a family, and they are therefore often singled out for special protection. The stranger is not to be wronged or oppressed, and the widow and orphan are not to be afflicted, on pain of God's appropriately avenging wrath ("your wives shall become widows and your children fatherless"). The sense of the directness and immediacy of God's relationship is remarkable. There is also sensitive discernment of the relationship between Israel's Egyptian experience and her proper treatment of a sojourner (vs. 21), an insight which appears again in 23:9 (see comment).

Verses 25-27 continue with admonitions on other aspects of Covenant life. "If *you* lend money to any of *my* people" (this is God's *torah*), you do so not as a creditor, exacting interest, but (such is the implication) out of compassion (see vs. 27) for a Covenant brother (compare Deut. 23:19-20; and Lev. 25:25-28). The garment offered to secure the loan "is his only covering" against the cold of the night and may not therefore be retained overnight. Again the Lord himself, who is compassionate, is an immediate party to the relationship between the lender and the poor.

Some interpreters say that verse 28 presupposes the institution of monarchy. This is hardly so; but in any case the prohibition gives support and protection to authority, divine and human, and it shows an awareness of the potential threat to community order inherent in the very utterance of contempt. Elsewhere (Lev. 24:16) the death sentence is imposed for the most extreme verbal blast against God, that is, blaspheming "the name of the LORD."

Verses 29-31 turn to cultic requirements. Verse 29b has been taken as evidence that ancient Israel at one time believed that God demanded the sacrifice of a first-born son. This is most unlikely. The *willingness* to offer the son, in some unprescribed ritual act which would symbolize that willingness, is here called for (see 13:2, 12, 15). The mainstream of the Israelite faith, from Moses through the prophets (see, for example, Micah 6:7) and on into post-exilic Judaism, persisted in unqualified repudiation of literal human sacrifice.

It was an old taboo, common among shepherd peoples, that animals of the flock which had been killed by wild beasts could not be eaten (in the primitive belief that the evil inherent in the attacking animals would be transferred to the eater). But characteristically, the old practice is given theological significance in Israel (vs. 31). You are mine, says the Lord, "consecrated to me"; and you may not *therefore* play the unworthy role of scavengers to the beasts of creation.

In 23:1-9 the Covenant Code gives its most eloquent instruction on the theme of justice. Verses 1-3 are surely part of the broad *torah* made succinct in the Decalogue's prohibition "You shall not bear false witness . . ." (20:16; see the comment). With great sensitivity the changes on the theme are rung, with admonitions against a false report; against false witness with malicious intent, entered into with a wicked accomplice; against the larger company's (the mob's) headstrong purpose to pervert justice; and against the tendency to temper justice on behalf of the poor (since Israelite *torah* itself exhibits this partiality, let the witness always be true). Leviticus 19:15 warns also against partiality to the great:

> "You shall do no injustice in judgment; you shall not be partial to the poor or defer to the great, but in righteousness shall you judge your neighbor."

The principle of justice, but especially of justice qualified with mercy, continues to be the theme in the verses that follow. Verses 4-5 are no less concerned than verses 1-3 with the perversion of right. Here what might pervert justice is one's reaction to one's "enemy," to the neighbor one would happily see removed to a far country. He and his animals must be treated with justice, righteousness, and compassion. That he and you are at enmity in no way qualifies your obligations under Covenant *torah*. The essential theme is passionately sounded elsewhere in the Bible (for example, in Prov. 25:21-22; Job 31:29; Matt. 5:43-48).

Verses 6 and 7 return to the particular concern of the opening verses of the chapter, with the added word of the Lord: "*I* will not acquit the wicked" even if—such is the inference—by your false witness *you* do. Verse 8 outlaws the use of that all-pervading instrument for the perversion of justice, the bribe, which "blinds the officials" and subverts righteousness. Deuteronomy 16: 19-20 records the Old Testament's most eloquent statement in this whole regard:

> "You shall not pervert justice; you shall not show partiality; and you shall not take a bribe, for a bribe blinds the eyes of the wise and subverts the cause of the righteous. Justice, and only justice, you shall follow, that you may live and inherit the land which the LORD your God gives you."

Verse 9 again (as 22:21) holds up justice with particular regard for the "stranger," that is, the sojourner or the non-native who is now a resident temporarily, semi-permanently, or permanently. The point of appeal in support of the admonition is again (as it is also in 22:21) the principle of identification—you, Israel, know what it is to be a sojourner! But the matter is put here with the most acute sensitivity, saying literally:

A sojourner shall you not oppress; for as for you (the form is plural and emphatic), you know the heart (!) of a sojourner because you were yourselves sojourners in the land of Egypt.

In the light of what is said here, it is not surprising that in the subsequent development of *torah* it was declared of the sojourner, "You shall love him as yourself" (Lev. 19:34).

Verses 10-19 are concerned exclusively with matters of religious practice. During the Sabbath *year* the land was to have rest, in order to give aid to the poor; any uncultivated yield was to go first to them, and after them to the wild beasts. But surely also, implicitly, the purpose of such a commandment was to symbolize and memorialize God's ownership of the land (vss. 10-11).

Verses 12 and 13 deal with the Sabbath day (see also 20:8-11; Deut. 5:12-15). They are marked by a characteristically gentle consideration for ox and ass, servants and aliens. There appears here also, in defense of the Sabbath, a warning against the temptation to throw it over in "the names of other gods."

The three major annual feasts of the religious year are dealt with in verses 14-19. The feast of "unleavened bread" ("passover" in 34:25) commemorated the exodus from Egypt (vss. 14-15; see comment on 11:1—13:16). The feast of "harvest" ("weeks" in 34:22; Deuteronomy 16:10, 16; or "Pentecost," since it was observed fifty days after the beginning of the Feast of Unleavened Bread in Acts 2:1; 20:16; I Corinthians 16:8; or the "first fruits of wheat harvest," also in Exodus 34:22) celebrated the first harvests of the fields, ready in Palestine in April. This continued to be observed as an agricultural festival in the Old Testament; in later Judaism it became associated with the giving of the Law. The third feast, that of "ingathering" (so also in 34:22; but in Deuteronomy 16:13-16, the feast of "tabernacles" or "booths"), celebrated the grape vintage in the fall. These "three times in the year shall all your males appear before the Lord GOD" (vs. 17). In ancient Israel—as is still true to a considerable extent in Judaism—women played no role in the cultic festivals, save that they were in no sense excluded from accompanying the male members of the family to the sanctuary and supporting the cultic ceremony with their presence (see I Sam. 1). In this connection one must also recall the very significant roles in the total life of Israel played by women like Miriam, the sister of Moses

(15:20-21), Deborah, one of Israel's most notable pre-monarchic leaders (Judges 5), and Huldah, the influential prophetess of the seventh century B.C., whose personal-professional sanction set in motion the sweeping reforms of King Josiah (II Kings 22:14-20).

Verses 18-19, to which 34:25-26 is almost identical, give four specifications for the regulation of sacrifice. Verse 18 surely has reference to the Passover (as in 34:25), which is here known as the Feast of Unleavened Bread, warning against carrying the Passover celebration beyond its appointed day. Verse 19a reiterates verse 16. Verse 19b may or may not have had a human motivation; the matter continues to be debated by interpreters. The prohibition (occurring also in 34:26 and Deut. 14:21) came to be interpreted as excluding *any* mixture of milk and meat, and, at least in later rabbinic Judaism, was understood as a repudiation of gluttony. No such prohibition, whatever the motivation, appears in extrabiblical law.

Exodus 23:20-33. The concluding section in the block formed by chapters 22-23 is of a markedly different character from the two preceding groups of casuistic laws and apodictic *torah*. But the common theme of conduct and responsibility continues, although there is no explicit reference to what has gone before. Sharp attention is given to what ostensibly lies immediately ahead for Israel; that is, the taking and the disposition of the land of Canaan and its inhabitants, and Israel's settling in that land. In their present form these verses reveal at points the characteristic vocabulary and style of the Deuteronomic editors (compare, for example, Deut. 7:1-5); but the basic structure of this speech of the Lord (probably verses 20-22, 25b-28, and 31a) may be as old as the tenth century and may rest upon an oral form of still earlier date. The predicted limits of the land (verse 31: from the Reed Sea—in this case undoubtedly the Gulf of Aqabah—to the Mediterranean, and across the desert eastward to the Euphrates River) represent approximately the extent of the Israelite kingdom in the tenth century, at the close of David's reign—the peak period of Israel's political power.

The speech also includes in its present form some indication of the relatively slow progress of the occupation and acquisition of Canaan: "Little by little I will drive them out from before you" (vs. 30); and it refers to some force, designated as "hornets" (vs. 28; see Deut. 7:20 and Joshua 24:12; see also "the fly" and "the bee" in Isa. 7:18). This force, perhaps unwittingly, assists in Israel's conquest of the land.

Whatever the original date of these words of the Lord in the Covenant Code, they come firmly and timelessly together in one eloquent affirmation of the Covenant relationship, of God's continuing gracious purposes in Israel, and in a statement of the response that is appropriate for Israel—a single, uncompromised trust in the Lord. The mention of the guiding, accompanying angel (vss. 20, 23; see also 14:19; Gen. 31:11 and 48:16) reflects the general tendency in Israel and in the Old Testament to avoid the assumption that there could be a direct revelation of the *totality* of the Person of the Lord. The angel functions as the Word—that is, as the revelation of God which is sufficient for and appropriate to the particular moment of history. "My name is in him," declares the Lord (vs. 21). It is, then, in God's Name, in the representation of his essential Person, that the land is theirs. Sustaining food, sweet water, days without illness, births without accident, parental love fulfilled and without frustration, and a satisfying length of years (vss. 25-26)—these are the terms in which the abundant life is offered in the Covenant relationship in which God creates a people and in which a people serve him in faithfulness. The specific, detailed, and even arduous ordering of Covenant life which begins at 20:18 is thus gently and warmly rounded out with a moving affirmation of the powers, gifts, and commitment of the Senior Party to the Covenant. If all the preceding Covenant Code is the recitation of Israel's obligations under the Covenant, this conclusion reassuringly sets forth God's participating responsibilities. And if the detailed prescriptions of the Code seem difficult of fulfillment, what will a man give for such fulfilled existence, lived out in trust and love of God?

The Sealing of Covenant (24:1-18)

God and People (24:1-11)

The term "tradition" is used to describe the total work, over a span of five, six, or seven centuries, of collecting, arranging, and editing the tremendous variety of materials which make up the present Old Testament record. Exodus 24 shows more clearly than many other passages the fact that tradition's work is a composite labor. Two ceremonies which ratify and seal the Covenant are described here. The chapter apparently records two different "memories" of the way in which the Covenant was formerly closed—memories which originally were preserved independently of one another, finally to be brought together and combined in this process which we call "tradition."

The earliest understanding of Covenant in Israel saw God as the initiator of Covenant and, in the act of Covenant-making, or Covenant-sealing, as the active member in the two-party pact. Covenant is of his ordering alone; and it is he who, in the rite of ratification, symbolizes his own commitment to the Covenant. This understanding of Covenant-making appears here in verses 1-2 and 9-11 (unfortunately in fragmented form, for more space is given to the later view of Covenant-making). Here God himself prepares a communion meal to which he invites Israel's leaders. Israel's function, as seen in this representation, is only to eat: it is God who gives the food and who, in giving it, commits himself to the Covenant.

Such an act of Covenant-sealing appears, of course, not only at Sinai or in the narratives which make up the total Sinai tradition. It also appears in connection with the patriarchs and most graphically in connection with Abraham in Genesis 15 where the point is made, with even greater emphasis, that God is the active party of the Covenant irrevocably committing himself (compare Jer. 34:18) in a binding ceremony of ratification, while Israel, in the person of Abraham, only stands by.

In this understanding of Covenant, Israel's remarkable faith is attested. It is God's Covenant, not ours; it is dependent for its continuing existence upon him, not upon us. He is the Senior Partner who has voluntarily and unequivocally committed himself. And so, in Israel's bleakest and most dismal hours, faith in the ultimate fulfillment of Covenant purpose, hope, and promise was never abandoned. That faith survived every catastrophe, to be reformulated as the New or the Renewed Covenant (see Jer. 31:31-34). And that same faith identified Jesus Christ as the final and complete fulfillment of Covenant, old and new (see Matt. 26:28; Mark 14:24; I Cor. 11:25; Heb. 9:15-22).

We know that covenants in the ancient East were of several kinds. Some covenants, in fact, involved simply the commitment of the senior to the junior member; others required a decisive mutuality, the acceptance of formally defined obligation, and appropriate ceremonial ratification of mutual covenant by both parties. In the patriarchal narratives the rite of circumcision is designated as the rite by which a covenant is sealed (Gen. 17). Here in Exodus the Decalogue and the Covenant Code are identified as Israel's obligation under the Covenant, and the rite which is described in Exodus 24:3-8 is seen as the appropriate ceremony which enacts and symbolizes Israel's acceptance of and commitment to such a covenant.

In all the biblical forms of Covenant-making, blood plays a decisive symbolic role. In Genesis 15 God (symbolized by the flaming torch) passes between the severed (bloody) halves of sacrificial animals. Circumcision (Gen. 17; Exod. 4:24-26; Joshua 5:2-7), whatever else it symbolizes, involves the shedding of blood. The ceremony described in Exodus 24:3-8 binds people to God as blood is sprinkled on people (vs. 8) and on the altar (vs. 6). The ancient ceremony of a communion meal bound guest to host as they ate together of meat (necessarily involving the "sacrifice" of the animal and the shedding of blood). In the New Covenant, of course, the same essential symbolism appears (Matt. 26:28 and I Cor. 11:25). But of the two types of ceremony illustrated in Exodus 24, the New Testament clearly puts its emphasis upon the older of the two. "God so loved the world that he gave . . ."; and we, the junior partners in this Covenant, witness his commitment, made in love and grace. We have only to receive the gift and to respond to the giving of the gift (his ratification of Covenant) with the same kind of love.

God and Moses (24:12-18)

In the opening verses of chapter 24 Aaron and his two sons, Nadab and Abihu (see Lev. 10:1-3), plus "seventy of the elders of Israel" are given significant roles (24:1, 9). In the scene described in verses 12-18 Joshua is introduced (vs. 13; see 33:11; Joshua 1:1).

The Law given on Sinai is vested with such authority as to give rise to the repeated assertion that God himself wrote it (see 31:18, "written with the finger of God," and 34:1; but contrast 34:27-28). But this is really not the primary motif of the scene described here. The purpose here is to round out the section beginning with chapter 19 and, at the same time, to set the stage for the long Priestly section which follows in chapters 25-31, having to do with plans for institutionalizing all that has occurred in the making of the Covenant. The section serves to indicate again the absolutely unique role of Moses in Israelite history. It also emphasizes the fact that in the practice of Israel's faith in succeeding generations, each development of form and content came with the authority of God directly mediated through Moses.

THE PLANS OF INSTITUTION

Exodus 25:1—31:18

Chapters 25-31 occur in the midst of an extended block of material which has been organized around the particular place, Sinai. What are commonly designated as "Yahwistic" and "priestly" elements of tradition have been combined in this large block which extends from Exodus 19 all the way through Numbers 10:10. The "non-priestly" sections are Exodus 19-24, and 32-34. The material that is essentially "priestly" (chs. 25-31 and 35-40) affirm not only that all *torah* (instruction) comes down to Israel with the authority of Moses and Sinai, but also the total *form* of Israel's institution of religion as well.

Introduction (25:1-9)

The whole section begins with the affirmation, "The LORD *said* to Moses . . ." This forms a connection with the preaching material (see 24:12) and also emphasizes the divine sanction for what is to follow. The command is to build the sanctuary "that I may dwell in their midst" (vs. 8). The sense of the sanctuary's utter sacredness is attested also in the statement that the *plans* for the Tabernacle and its total furnishings originate here in the Sinai tradition. The material means for executing the plans are to come "from every man whose heart makes him willing" to give (vs. 2; see also 35:21-22).

The Ark (25:10-22)

In the religion of Israel the Ark was the most sacred object. The "cubit" measure was the length of a forearm, standardized in English measure as eighteen inches. Accordingly, on the assumption that this must also have been the approximate length of a cubit in the Old Testament, the Ark must have measured about 45 by 27 by 27 inches (vs. 10). It contained the tables of the Law (vs. 16; I Kings 8:9; Deut. 10:5) and a pot of manna and Aaron's rod (Heb. 9:4; see Exod. 16:33 and Num. 17:10). The

Ark, of course, symbolized God's Presence and had a place, both in the Tabernacle and later in the Temple, at the innermost and holiest location. The "mercy seat," a rectangular plate on top of the Ark and of similar dimensions, underscores the fact that the Ark represents the Presence; for at either end of the mercy seat and facing one another were cherubim (winged creatures of varying form and size) between whom or above whom was the Presence (vs. 22; see Num. 7:89; I Sam. 4:4; II Sam. 6:2; II Kings 19:15; Pss. 80:1 and 99:1; Isa. 37:16). Cherubim, perhaps of Mesopotamian origin, were images with winged animal bodies and human heads. Two cherubim, each fifteen feet high, stood in Solomon's Temple on either side of the Ark within the Holy of Holies (I Kings 6:23). The mercy seat reminds us that a profound awareness of human sinfulness was characteristic of even the "priestly" strand of Israel's tradition. In the Holy of Holies, at the center of the center, there stood the seat of God's *mercy*.

Table and Lampstand (25:23-40)

The prevailing tendency in these detailed plans is toward the elaboration of the forms and symbols of the religion of Israel. For example, the original Ark, probably dating from Mosaic times, must have been a very simple wooden box. The plans of institution which come down to us probably tended to read back into pre-monarchic and Mosaic times the elaborated forms which were characteristic of the days of the kingdoms and even of post-exilic Judaism. The table is designed to hold "the bread of the Presence"; but when we first encounter this bread in historical narrative (I Sam. 21:1-6) there is no mention of a table. In any case, we may be confident that this table, profusely decorated with gold, represents an elaborate development of the most simple original arrangement. The lampstand with seven branches must be understood in the same way. This work of pure gold (vs. 31) weighing more than a hundred pounds (vs. 39; a "talent" exceeded a hundred pounds in weight) was a relatively late device (in 27:20-21 there is only a single lamp for lighting the sanctuary); perhaps it was even post-exilic (around 500 B.C.).

The Tabernacle (26:1-37)

A detailed discussion of the exceedingly complex problems involved in the plans for the Tabernacle is not justified in limited space. One must be content with the observation that what is described here bears no direct relationship to any historical Israelite sanctuary of which we have knowledge. Memories of a Mosaic tent of meeting suitable for a nomadic group may be deeply and, at the present, inextricably imbedded in the specifications. Moreover, it is certain that the form of Solomon's Temple built in the tenth century B.C. influenced the present description to some degree. But a reconstruction according to the specifications here produces a composite and imaginary structure with a broad frame (vss. 15-25) unreconcilable in certain respects with the tent and its drape coverings (vss. 1-14). There is no reason to doubt the existence of a portable sanctuary, a "tent of meeting"—not of man and man, but of man with God—as Israel's earliest religious center. But it is impossible to reconstruct that sanctuary from the present description.

Altar, Court, Night Lamp (27:1-21)

The entire section which deals with the plans of institution is carefully ordered. We start in the Holy of Holies with the Ark and mercy seat, that is, in the most sacred room, farthest removed from the entrance. The furnishings (table and lampstand) in the main body of the sanctuary, the space from the Holy of Holies to the entrance, are then defined; and then as we move outward, the very structure itself is described. Now in chapter 27 we are in the court before the sanctuary, in which the dominant object is the great altar (see 40:29). Again the plan corresponds to Solomon's Temple (II Kings 16:10-15), although this Tabernacle altar (3 cubits high by 5 by 5) has been appropriately scaled down (from 10 cubits high by 20 by 20). Perhaps in Tabernacle practice, and certainly in later Temple practice, this was the main altar, the "altar of burnt offering" (see 30:28 and 31:9), or the "bronze altar" (38:30 and 39:39). The horns at the four corners (vs. 2) could hardly have been on an altar in Mosaic times, since these are clearly of Canaanite design and origin. The court (vss. 9-19) must also reflect the later Temple pattern, since in the nature of a simple sanctuary such an elaborate and sharply defined area is improbable. Verse 19 apparently concludes the idealized plan for Israel's sanctuary, for the subject turns—somewhat irrelevantly but with pertinence to what follows—to the matter of keeping the (single) sanctuary lamp. Later this lamp is to be kept perpetually burning (Lev. 24:1-3), but here it is a lamp to be lighted each night and to burn in the sanctuary throughout the night.

The Priests: Apparel and Ordination (28:1—29:46)

Among the detailed items of the priests' wardrobe, the "ephod" (28:4, 6-14) is something of a puzzle. The term must have applied in the Old Testament to two different kinds of objects. In Judges 8:24-27; 17:5; 18:14; and Hosea 3:4 the ephod is clearly an image of some sort, and it is possible that the same object is referred to in I Samuel 2:28; 23:9; and 30:7. But the boy Samuel *wore* the ephod at the ancient sanctuary at Shiloh (I Sam. 2:18). It further appears that this garment contained (in a pocket?) sacred lots used to determine the will of the Lord (I Sam. 14:3, 36-42 and 23:9-12).

Anyone eager to pursue the matter of the priests' consecration and ordination will consult in detail Leviticus 1-7. Indeed, what is given in Exodus concerning these sacred rites is demonstrably dependent upon the prescriptions in Leviticus, and must therefore, at least in its present form, be later than the Levitical material. The prominent place and singular attention given to the *high* priest (in the person of Aaron) probably further points up the exilic or post-exilic origin of the present text; there is no conclusive evidence that the office of high priest in this highly specialized sense existed prior to the Exile. The section dealing with the priests' apparel and ordination is concluded in 29:42b-46 with moving words which reflect the theology always underlying the Priestly perspective. The sometimes formidable Priestly structure, elaborately prescribed in cultic form, equipment, and personnel, is *not* an end in itself, as sometimes it may appear and as, in interpretation, it has often been alleged. It is testimony to the fact of God's continuing Presence in Israel and to the means of realization of that Presence:

> ". . . I will dwell among the people of Israel, and will be their God. And they shall know that I am the LORD their God, who brought them forth out of the land of Egypt that I might dwell among them; I am the LORD their God" (29:45-46).

Miscellaneous Additions (30:1—31:11)

To the foregoing plans of institution—themselves a composite

work drawn from an earlier and a later Priestly source—still later
Priestly editors have added what they deemed to be pertinent
instructions with respect to a variety of items. The incense altar
(30:1-10), not to be confused with the main altar of burnt offering (27:1-8), may possibly have been employed in pre-
prophetic Israel (that is, before the mid-eighth century B.C.);
but if so it was abandoned, to appear again in post-exilic Judaism.
The census (30:11-16), prescribed here for the purpose of fixing
a sanctuary tax, but always undertaken with some apprehension
of incurring God's anger (hence, "a ransom" to avoid any evil
consequences; vs. 12, see II Sam. 24), is further explained as
atonement money—it is to bring "the people of Israel to re-
membrance before the LORD." The bronze basin ("laver," 30:
17-21) stands between the front of the sanctuary and the altar
of incense and is designed for the ceremonial purification of the
priests. To this assorted collection of items, recipes are now added
for making anointing oil (30:22-33) and incense (30:34-38).
Finally, responsibility is assigned to peculiarly gifted men to carry
out all these plans of institution (31:1-11; compare the parallel
account in 35:30—36:7).

Reiteration of the Sabbath Commandment; and Conclusion (31:12-18)

This "priestly" statement of the Sabbath law is absolute and
unequivocal. Violation incurs the death penalty (stated twice in
verse 14 and again in verse 15). The Sabbath is the most characteristic sign and perpetual attestation of the Covenant. Its observance is the affirmation of the peculiar relationship of grace
between God and Israel and of the fact that it is God himself
who sanctifies the people (vs. 13). It is also the appropriate acknowledgment that the Lord made heaven and earth; it is the
"sign for ever" between the Creator and the people of Israel
that *all* is his (vs. 17).

The extended Priestly section on the plans of institution (25:
1—31:18) is concluded with a notice which also admirably
serves to introduce the next major section (chs. 32-34). It is the
implied connection of all of these plans with the occasion when
God spoke to Moses on Mount Sinai. They have the same authority as the giving of the tables of the Law, "written with the
[very] finger of God."

THE DENIAL AND RENEWAL OF COVENANT
Exodus 32:1—34:35

For a discussion of the composite nature of this section, its general "Yahwistic" cast, and its relationships to materials before and after, which make up its total context, one should refer to the Introduction. These chapters are dominated by the figure and role of Moses. The present form of the narrative has certainly in some measure been shaped by Israel's annual celebration of the Sinai Covenant, as each year the making of Covenant was re-enacted, and the structure of the Covenant itself renewed. The *form* of celebration echoes the historical form of the sojourn at Sinai; nevertheless, Israel's interest in the original event was predominantly in its ever-present meaning. The image of Moses, then, is not only the result of historical recollection, it is also the result of long years of meditation on the total significance of his life and work through the succeeding generations of Israel's life.

The Golden Calf (32:1-35)

Moses is on Sinai, now himself as mysterious and unapproachable as that Presence of the Lord which he alone may confront and as that Word of the Lord which he alone may hear. The impatient people, to whom the reality of Moses and of God has become only a memory, remember the widespread pagan representation of deity in the form of a calf (probably a young bull, denoting primarily the strength of reproductive power and fertility, natural and human). With Aaron's consent and counsel, they make what they take to be a representation of "the LORD" in this form, and hold a full-fledged cultic celebration to "the LORD" (vs. 5).

God's immediate repudiation of Israel for this breach of Covenant is directly conveyed in his Word to Moses, communicating the sense of ruptured relationship, profound and powerful:

> "Go down; for *your* people, whom *you* brought up out of the land of Egypt, have corrupted themselves" (vs. 7).

Then comes the warning against interference while judgment is sent:

"Now therefore let me alone, that . . . I may consume them."

Then we hear the thematic note:

". . . of you [Moses] I will make a great nation" (vs. 10).

But Moses will not entertain this complimentary proposal even by mentioning it. Instead he makes successful (vs. 14) intercession on Israel's behalf, as it were reminding God that Israel is his people, whose destruction would frustrate the glory of the Exodus (vss. 11-12) and constitute a breach of God's promise to the patriarchs (vs. 13).

Moses descends the mountain, carrying the two stone tablets inscribed with the Decalogue ("the writing was the writing of God," vs. 16), and sees what has occurred (vs. 19; note the sudden reappearance of Joshua, vs. 17; compare 24:13). In fury Moses breaks the tablets, devastatingly symbolizing the fact that Israel has in the same way just shattered the Covenant.

It all happened "at the foot of the mountain" (vs. 19). It was here that Moses first came with Jethro's flock; here he first knew the piercing of the shell of his existence by the Word of the Lord, coming out of the undiminished, unconsumed burning bush. To the same foot of the same mountain Moses had brought Israel. Here a people redeemed only yesterday out of slavery had acknowledged the Lord as the Shatterer of their own tight little prison, and had entered into a Covenant with him, accepting his commitment to them and reciting their own vows of faithfulness. Here, at the foot of the mountain, they now brazenly denied the reality of their Encounter, repudiated their Emancipator, and shamelessly broke their vows. Here, at the foot of the mountain, then, Moses cast into the moral rubble the tables of the testimony, already in effect reduced to powder and ashes.

When Moses confronts Aaron as the one on whom responsibility clearly falls, Aaron at once gives an emphatic disclaimer, blaming the people, and for himself offering an excuse which forever ranks with the best and the most ridiculous of its kind: "I said to them," explains Aaron,

" 'Let any who have gold take it off'; so they gave it to me, and I threw it into the fire, and there came out this calf" (vs. 24).

Behind this whole incident and the account of the slaughter which follows (vss. 27-28), we can detect the seriousness of the prohibition of images in Israel and the theological maturity and perception which it represents. At the same time and in the light of the full biblical revelation we recognize what seems to be a mingling of the human word with the divine Word in the command of indiscriminate slaughter (see also vs. 35).

Along with this narrative of judgment there is sounded, in verses 31-32, the note of Moses' moving intercession, to be ranked with the greatest prayers ever preserved. Here also is the response of the Word of grace (vs. 34a); but it is given along with the firm reminder that the Lord will, when the occasion demands, make himself known as Judge (vs. 34b).

Many Old Testament students hold that the present narrative was created as a condemnation (with Mosaic-Sinaitic "authority") of the use of bull images at the two chief sanctuaries of northern Israel, Dan and Bethel, beginning late in the tenth century when the united Israelite kingdom was split (I Kings 12: 28-29). But at the later time the image was *not* equated with the Deity; rather, it was deemed to be the Lord's throne or footstool. It may be that tradition reinterpreted the present story in the light of this seeming heresy; but there is no reason to deny that the story was already in existence earlier in the tenth century and that, in fact, image representation began in the beginning of Israel's life as a people, in the first, Mosaic chapter of that life. Israelite worship *always* ran the danger of confusing the throne or the pedestal of the footstool of the Lord (the image of the calf or bull) with the Lord himself.

The Lord and Moses (33:1—34:9)

Chapter 33 opens with the Lord's Word still sounding in reaction to the broken Covenant: "You [Moses] and the people whom *you* have brought up out of the land of Egypt" are to get out of here and move on to the land. But it is still the *promised* land; and God declares, "I will drive out" those who impede your settlement in the land. An inconsistent and negative note is, however, sounded in verse 3.

This note of ambivalence plays a role in the plot. God's Word has been given. That Word cannot be broken. But Israel has behaved in flagrant defiance and abuse of all that was implicit in the Covenant Word; from any human point of view God is justified in having no more to do with Israel, indeed in withdrawing himself for Israel's own protection, since to stay among them in wrath would be to destroy them (vs. 5). This tension and duality serve in the delineation of the character of Moses, since it is the person of Moses and the intercession and faith of Moses which are responsible for the resolution of the ambivalence.

In hope of appeasing the divine anger, the Israelites "stripped themselves of their ornaments, from Mount Horeb [Sinai] onward" (vs. 6).

In this narrative, more clearly than in any previous reference, the tent of meeting is the place where the Lord may be found (vs. 7). The use of the two terms "tent of meeting" and "tabernacle" leaves the reader in doubt as to whether they are the same structure or represent different arrangements. Chapters 29 (vss. 4, 10, 11, 30, 32, 42, 44) and 30 (vss. 16, 18, 20, 36), for example, employ only the first term (see also 27:21 and 28:43) and clearly identify the tent with the Tabernacle. In chapter 33 it *may* be that the tent of meeting is envisaged as a provisional arrangement, a substitute tabernacle for the duration of God's withholding his own direct Presence from Israel: God meets directly only with Moses in the tent of meeting—and that "face to face" (vs. 11; but note also the contrast in verse 20, apparently stemming from another of the sources employed by tradition in the shaping of the present account). In subsequent references the identity or virtual identity of the "tent of meeting" and the "tabernacle" must be assumed (35:21; 38:8, 30; see especially 39:40 and ch. 40).

In chapter 33 the uniqueness of Moses is defined in terms of the uniqueness of his relationship to the Lord. Israel owes her existence to the Lord, to be sure, but also to Moses, without whose intercession and intervention the Covenant enterprise would, to all intents and purposes, have been dissolved. This is testimony and tribute to the absolutely incomparable Moses. He goes alone to the tent of meeting for a Meeting—*the* Meeting— while all Israel stands in awe and reverence (vs. 8). The Lord follows, and all Israel worships, "every man at his tent door" (vss. 9-10). It is face-to-face Meeting. Moses is represented as speaking with such power as to persuade the Lord of the wisdom of his words and to gain a reversal of the divine decision to withhold the immediate Presence of the Lord from Israel (vss. 12-

17). And the Lord bestows on Moses words of rare (and in the light of the New Testament, strikingly significant) occurrence: "I know you by *name*" (vss. 12, 17; compare Matt. 1:21-23; 16:13-20); "you have . . . found favor in my sight" (vss. 12, 17; compare Mark 1:10-11; Luke 2:40); "I will give you rest" (vs. 14; compare Matt. 11:28); and "This very thing that you have spoken I will do" (vs. 17; compare Matt. 10:32; Luke 12:8; John 16:23).

Finally, in marked contrast to the tent-of-meeting Meeting ("face to face," vs. 11; see Num. 12:8; Deut. 34:10), a request by Moses to behold the Lord's "glory" is granted (vss. 18-23; compare *and contrast* Elijah's great hour on the holy mountain in I Kings 19). The quality and meaning of the Glory is suggested in the coupling of the proclamation of the divine name, "The LORD" (vs. 19; 34:6), with the passing by of the Glory. The words "goodness," "gracious," and "mercy" (vs. 19; see 34:6-7) also emphasize the nature of the Glory. Implicit, of course, in this concept is the fact of God's forgiveness of Israel, won through the intercession and devotion of Moses, and assured now in the passing Glory of goodness, grace, and mercy. The description of the passing by of the Glory rounds out the intimate scene between God and Moses (34:6-9). It expands the theme of the graciousness of the Lord (see Joel 2:13; Jonah 4:2) and affirms the appropriate humility of Moses before this revelation of the nature of the Lord. The prayer of Moses constitutes a fine summary of all that has gone before in chapters 32 and 33. "If now I [Moses] *have* [in very fact] found favor in thy sight," then

> ". . . let the Lord . . . go in the midst of us, although it is a stiff-necked people; and pardon our iniquity and our sin, and take us for thy inheritance" (34:9).

It is important that in 34:1-8 the narrative returns to the stone tables of the Law which had been destroyed in Moses' wrath at the sight of the golden calf. Since Moses' marvelous vision of the Glory of the Lord serves also to symbolize the renewal of Covenant with Israel, the broken tablets must be replaced. These verses supply the logical and necessary prelude to the remaking of the Covenant, and repeat the basis of the relationship between God and man in the nature of God himself.

The Redefined Covenant (34:10-28)

The Covenant between the Lord, "merciful and gracious, slow to anger, and abounding in steadfast love and faithfulness" (34:6) and a forgiven Israel is instituted afresh. In the present text of Exodus 34 the content of the new Covenant Law differs from the old as phrased in the Decalogue (Exod. 20). Following an introductory speech of the Lord, which declares the marvels he is about to perform, and which warns against the temptations of Canaan and its religious institutions (vss. 10-13), a decalogue is again given. This, however, concentrates exclusively on concerns of the religion, and has therefore come to be known as the "Ritual Decalogue" (as over against what is often called the "Ethical Decalogue" of Exodus 20 and Deuteronomy 5):

I. You shall worship no other god, for the LORD, whose name is Jealous, is a jealous God (vs. 14; see 23:13).

II. You shall make for yourself no molten gods (vs. 17; see 20:23).

III. All that opens the womb is mine (vs. 19a; see 22:29b-30).

IV. All the first-born of your sons you shall redeem (vs. 20b; see 22:29b-30).

V. Six days you shall work, but on the seventh day you shall rest; in plowing time and in harvest you shall rest (vs. 21; see 23:12).

VI. Three times in the year shall all your males appear before the LORD God, the God of Israel (vs. 23; see 23:17 and comment).

VII. You shall not offer the blood of my sacrifice with leaven (vs. 25a; see 23:18a).

VIII. The sacrifice of the feast of the passover [shall not] be left until the morning (vs. 25b; see 23:18b).

IX. The first of the first fruits of your ground you shall bring to the house of the LORD your God (vs. 26a; see 23:19a).

X. You shall not boil a kid in its mother's milk (vs. 26b; see 23:19b).

The parallel references from the Covenant Code (Exod. 20-23; but especially 23:13-19) indicate that this religious decalogue is unique only in arrangement; and its present form is obviously an expansion of an original "ten words." How old may have been such an original ritual decalogue? Did these prescriptions first appear in the corpus of an extensive code (the Covenant Code of Exodus 20-23), to be distilled into briefer, decalogue form? Or was the cultic decalogue the original, and did its individual prescriptions subsequently become incorporated in the longer code? And how does it happen that there should be recorded an ethical decalogue as the content of the first tables of the Law, but a ritual decalogue for the second? Questions of this kind remain still without certain answer. It may be that in combining differing independent but parallel accounts of Sinai-Horeb and its Covenant, the record, without attempt at reconciliation, has brought together an older version (the nucleus of Exod. 32-34; "J") which preserved a ritual decalogue, and a somewhat later version ("E," having its place of origin in the north) which associates the ethical decalogue with the Covenant of the sacred mountain. Or it may have been that in the long process of preserving the tradition an original "J" decalogue, very closely parallel to the "E" decalogue of Exodus 20, may have been at some point displaced in Exodus 34 by the ritual decalogue which now appears there. This latter theory has the merit of suggesting that in the earlier formulation there was no inconsistency, but that in the record of the renewed Covenant the new decalogue on the new tablets was essentially the reproduction of the original tables.

Moses (34:29-35)

This section on the denial of and renewal of the Covenant (chs. 32-34) concentrates on the nature of God and magnifies his work. A theme for the whole block of material may be seen in 34:10, "It is a terrible thing that I will do with you." "Terrible," of course, is to be taken in the sense of "exciting" rather than "dreadful" or "horrible." It includes also the idea of awe and wonder. On the terrestrial plane and at the human level, however, the narrative concentrates on Moses, on his role vis-à-vis the Lord and Israel, and on his incomparable stature as intermediary between God and People.

Appropriately, then, the section closes with this extraordinary tribute by tradition—which is of course the tribute of all Israel—to Moses. By a combination of intercession and argument, he has gained for Israel full divine forgiveness. By the strength of his own person and in the power of his own commitment to the Lord, he returns again, descending the sacred mountain with the new tables of the Covenant Law in his hands. And he does not know—it is elsewhere insisted that "the man Moses was very meek, more than all men that were on the face of the earth" (Num. 12:3)—he does not know that his face is literally aglow, shining with the radiance of the very Presence of God!

This is the ultimate tribute. This is Israel's enduring estimate of Moses. The people live because the Lord gave life *out* of Egypt for the death that they lived *in* Egypt. By his Word (or his Hand, or his Presence) he brought them through the sea, sustained them in the wilderness, made Covenant with them at Sinai, forgave them their appalling denial of him, and renewed in mercy and grace the Covenant which they had broken. But by the means of what amazing human instrument was all of this the accomplishment of the Word of the Lord on behalf of Israel?

> . . . for the place on which you are standing is holy ground. Moses, Moses! Put off your shoes . . . I know the affliction of my people . . . Come, I will send you . . . I will be with you . . . I will be with your mouth . . . and I will bring you into the land.

> Come up to me on the mountain and I will give you the tables of stone . . . Go down; for your people have corrupted themselves . . . let me alone that my wrath may burn hot against them and I may consume them; but I will make of you a great nation . . . I will give you rest . . . you have found favor in my sight . . . I know you by name . . . Behold, I make [again!] a covenant. Before all your people I will do marvels . . . it is a terrible thing that I will do with you!

No comment can better convey the staggering impression of such a man upon other men—not simply in Israel but in the world of all time—than this account of the face of Moses, so brilliantly shining with the radiance of the very Presence of God that it could be unveiled only in the presence of the Presence.

This is Moses—by whose offices and through whose leadership and vision the Covenant was first made; against whose devoted commitment to Israel's life the Covenant was shamelessly denied; and by whose strength of faith and communion with the Lord, Israel was forgiven and the Covenant renewed and reinstituted.

THE ACT OF INSTITUTION

Exodus 35:1—40:38

There is little in this extended section which has not appeared earlier in Exodus, chapters 25-31. In the earlier section these elaborate instructions on the physical means, forms, nature, dimensions, and personnel of the institutional "plant" are recorded as *plans*, while here they are repeated as a record of actual construction.

Sabbath (35:1-3)

In view of the other Sabbath prescriptions which exhibit sensitivity, imagination, eloquence, and theological insight (16:23-30; 20:8-11; 31:13-17; Deut. 5:12-15), this is, relatively speaking, a prosaic rendering of the commandment. Missing especially is reference to the basis of the Sabbath in Creation or in the act of deliverance.

Introduction (35:4-29)

Here, as in 25:1-9, the emphasis is placed upon the spirit of the giver, the cordial, willing disposition of the one making the offering of help for the Tabernacle (see especially vss. 5, 21, 22, 26, 29). The Tabernacle is to be built now (according to the list of specifications which are recorded in summary fashion in verses 10-18) with the free offerings of gifts and services of all Israel.

On Staff and Material (35:30—36:7)

The parallel account in 31:1-11 is dependent upon, and therefore later than, the section here. Two men of particular gifts, Bezalel and Oholiab, are called to teach and to serve as chief designing engineers. Along with them, however, is to serve "every able man in whom the LORD has put ability" (36:1). Meanwhile, gifts of material were coming in such profusion as in fact to handicap the work; and Moses was compelled to call a halt to this vigorous response.

The Tabernacle and Its Furnishings (36:8—38:20)

Parallels for these sections will be found as follows:

the Tabernacle itself (36:8-38) in 26:1-37;
Ark, table, and lampstand (37:1-24) in 25:10-40;
incense altar (37:25-28) in 30:1-10;
incense and oil (37:29) in 30:22-38;
altar of burnt offering, the main altar (38:1-7) in 27:1-8;
bronze basin ("laver"; 38:8) in 30:17-21;
court (38:9-20) in 27:9-19.

Inventory of Services and Offerings (38:21-31)

This appears to be a very late editorial offering, and does not have a parallel elsewhere.

The Priests' Apparel (39:1-31)

With this section comparison should be made with 28:1-43. It can also be observed that the account in chapter 39 has nothing to parallel the offices of ordination described in chapter 29.

Moses' Approval of the Tabernacle (39:32-43)

The finished work is reviewed by Moses and the conclusion of the matter is set in language strongly reminiscent of the account of Creation, where "God saw everything that he had made, and behold, it was very good" (Gen. 1:31). Here

> Moses saw all the work, and behold, they had done it; as the LORD had commanded, so had they done it. And Moses blessed them (39:43).

The Erection and Meaning of the Tabernacle (40:1-38)

Moses saw the completed work, but with the parts as yet unassembled. Now all the components are appropriately joined and arranged—by Moses himself. And yet, as is consistent with the rest of Exodus, it is Moses acting in precise obedience to the command of the Lord. The Tabernacle, the prototype of the Temple, with authority and validation to be taken over into the Temple, is then in fact the creation of God, through the instrumentality of Moses. Seven (the sacred number) times the phrase of identification is reiterated—Moses did so-and-so, "as the LORD had commanded Moses" (verses 19, 21, 23, 25, 27, 29, 32). "So Moses finished the work" (vs. 33).

The indestructible faith of Israel speaks in the closing lines of Exodus. Tabernacle and Temple tangibly represent the Presence of the Lord, the reality of the Covenant, the power of the Covenant promise. This unit of the physical institution is the material symbol of the supremely significant relationship of Elector-elected, Chooser-chosen, of the Lord-Israel, of God-people:

> Then the cloud covered the tent of meeting, and the glory of the LORD filled the tabernacle. . . . For throughout all their journeys the cloud of the LORD was upon the tabernacle by day, and fire was in it by night, in the sight of all the house of Israel (40:34, 38).

In the Book of Exodus tradition has created an inspired masterpiece. We who come to it with faith find that it is also our history, our story, our *torah,* our institution—but all gathered up and fulfilled in him who even now brings us up out of Egypt into life with God. We can affirm with Exodus—and with greater conviction *because* of Exodus—that in all our journeys we are not alone, that when we look with faith, the Lord is himself even now "in the sight of all the house of Israel."